The Non-Designer's InDesign Book

Essential
design
techniques
for print
projects

Robin Williams

Peachpit Press
Berkeley
California

The Non-Designer's InDesign Book
ROBIN WILLIAMS

©2012 by Robin Williams

Peachpit Press
1249 Eighth Street
Berkeley, California 94710
510.524.2178   voice
510.524.2221   fax

Editor:	Nikki McDonald
Proofer:	Cathy Lane
Interior design and production:	Robin Williams
Index:	Robin Williams
Cover design and production:	John Tollett
Prepress:	David Van Ness

Layout and design samples from *Mothering Magazine* are used with permission from Peggy O'Mara, Laura Egley Taylor, and Melyssa Holik. Thank you!

Peachpit Press is a division of Pearson Education.

Find us on the web at www.peachpit.com.

To report errors, please send a note to errata@peachpit.com.

ISBN 13: 978-0-321-77284-8
ISBN 10:   0-321-77284-9

10 9 8 7 6 5 4 3 2 1

Printed and bound in the United States of America

Contents

These are some of the booklets I create every two months, in which I get to combine my passion for design with my passion for the Shakespearean works!

TheShakespearePapers.com

VASTIDITY

EXSUFFLICATE

FAP

SECTION III   Play with Graphics and Color

Illustrations by John Tollett

SECTION IV   Fun and Useful Extras

Backmatter

Illustrations by John Tollett

Introduction

I do everything in InDesign—letters to my 102-year-old Grandmother, recipes for friends, play lists for my Shakespeare reading groups, signage for events, dissertations for school. When I write a book, I write it directly in InDesign.

Booklets, banners, envelopes, door hangers, posters, flyers, postcards, business cards and letterhead, bookmarks, greeting cards, menus, note pads, rack cards, table tents, brochures, catalogs, newsletters, bookplates, books, packaging, tickets, labels . . . the possibilities are endless! And with the remarkable online printing sites where you can get professional color printing for unbelievable prices, it is immensely useful to know the basics of graphic design and how to use a page layout application such as InDesign. Or if you want to create product such as coffee mugs, t-shirts, hats, one-off posters, dog clothes, postage stamps, or even jewelry boxes, you can create and upload files to sites such as CafePress.com or Zazzle.com, then buy them for yourself or make them available to the public. Such a world we live in!

I have to assume you are motivated, so this book involves DISCOVERY and EXPLORATION. The basics are here, but I fully expect you to take the basics and run with them! This is not a manual, so it's up to you to explore settings you haven't worked with before, menu items that aren't mentioned in this book, etc. My hope is that you will feel confident, after following the tasks in this book, to take off on your own. Don't forget the Help files!

And if you plan to use Adobe's new web design application (as I write this book, the application is called Muse), you'll have a head start in designing web pages with it because it is very similar to InDesign.

So you see, all sorts of new worlds open up once you are adept at using a great tool for design! Go design something!

Robin

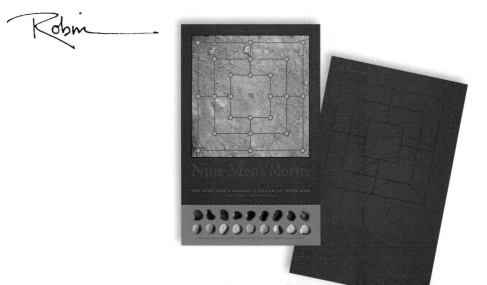

SECTION I

So... YOU want to learn INDESIGN

This section introduces you to the basics of working in InDesign, before getting to text frames and graphics. If you take the time to work through the few exercises in this section, you'll feel much more confident when you launch into any project.

Because InDesign is an advanced application, I expect that you know how to use your mouse and the windows; the difference between a single click and a double click; how to find, open, and save files; how to access contextual menus (right-click or Control-click on a Mac); and how to use your computer in general. But you probably know all those things already or you wouldn't be jumping into InDesign!

Type

is one of the most

eloquent means of expression

in every epoch of style.

Next to architecture,

it gives the most

characteristic portrait of a period

and the most severe testimony

of a nation's

intellectual status.

Peter Behrens
architect and designer, 1868–1940

Introduction to InDesign

The general way to use InDesign is to place some graphics on the page, get some text on the page, and design them into a piece. Putting the graphics and text on the page is the easy part—the fine-tuning is what takes time to master. This book merely gets you started in the right direction.

This primary chapter introduces you to a few of the background basics that you'll use in every project. It's not very exciting, but it's useful, and if it is useful, it is beautiful.

Document setup

As in any other program, to create a new document you go to the File menu and choose "New." In InDesign, you have a choice of creating a new Document (shown below), a Book (a file for managing individual chapter files in a book), or a Library (for easy access to items you use often; see page 196). If you don't have a new, blank document open yet, follow the steps below.

TASK 1   Make a new document

Any settings you make while creating a new document can always be changed, so don't worry too much about choosing the wrong thing.

1   From the File menu, choose "New," then "Document."

2   In the "Intent" option, make sure "Print" is chosen.

3   Let's make several pages to play on—enter 2 or 3 in the "Number of Pages" field.

4   If there's a check in the box for "Facing Pages," uncheck it.

5   Choose the "Page Size" option of "Letter," with a portrait (tall) "Orientation."

6   If the margins are 3p0 or .5 in. all the way around, leave them like that (or enter those numbers, if not).

7   Click OK. You should now have a single, untitled, blank page on the screen, as shown opposite.

8   **Save** this document into the folder of your choice, just as you do with all your other documents.

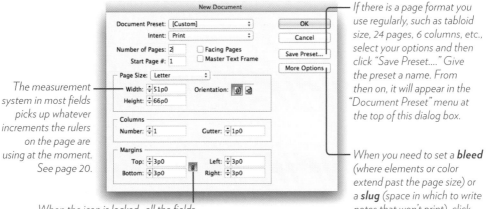

The measurement system in most fields picks up whatever increments the rulers on the page are using at the moment. See page 20.

When the icon is locked, all the fields will automatically change to match a number you enter in any one of them.

If there is a page format you use regularly, such as tabloid size, 24 pages, 6 columns, etc., select your options and then click "Save Preset...." Give the preset a name. From then on, it will appear in the "Document Preset" menu at the top of this dialog box.

*When you need to set a **bleed** (where elements or color extend past the page size) or a **slug** (space in which to write notes that won't print), click "More Options."*

Get to know the workspace

InDesign opens your document in a **workspace,** as shown below. A workspace determines which panels are open for you and where they are placed, your ruler settings, what is visible in the Control panel, etc. You can customize the **workspace** endlessly and save various workspaces for different sorts of projects.

For now, we're going to use the workspace that InDesign has already created, called "Essentials." If that's not what you see at the moment, go to the Window menu at the top of the screen, choose "Workspace," and then choose "Essentials." It will look like the screen below.

*Each document has its own **tab.***

*Horizontal **ruler.** See page 10.*

*You can also choose a different **workspace** from this menu (if the Application bar is showing).*

Application bar.
Control panel. See page 9.

Tools panel. See page 9.

*Vertical **ruler.** See page 10.*

Pasteboard. The pasteboard is for storing things on. It doesn't print.

Page number. Click the arrows to go back, forward, or get a menu of pages to choose from.

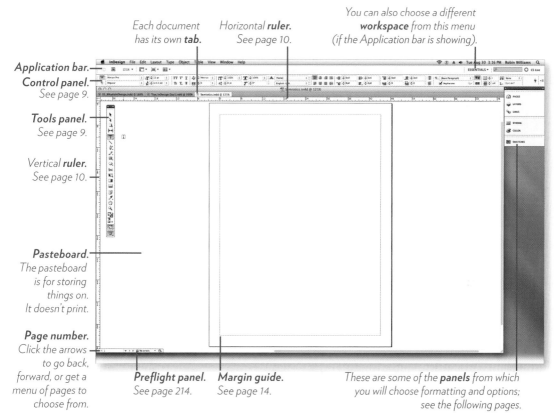

Preflight panel. See page 214.

Margin guide. See page 14.

*These are some of the **panels** from which you will choose formatting and options; see the following pages.*

Delete the Application bar: The Application bar takes up a lot of room on the screen. Everything in the bar can be accessed from a menu or the Tools panel. If you want to get rid of it, go to the Window menu and uncheck "Application bar."

When you're familiar with InDesign and have figured out how you like to arrange the tools and panels on your screen, you can save your own arrangement: Go to the Window menu, the "Workspace" command, choose "New Workspace," and give it a name. Whenever your panels get all messy, choose your workspace again and all will be returned to how you like it.

The panels

It can make you crazy if you don't understand how the panels work. If you're proficient in Photoshop or Illustrator, you are probably comfortable working with panels, so skip this section. If you've never worked with them before, take a few minutes to familiarize yourself because you're going to be working with panels every minute in InDesign.

To open panels if they're not already on the screen, get them from the Window menu or the Type menu. Learn their keyboard shortcuts so you can open them quickly.

TASK 2   Open the docked panels on the side of the screen

If you just opened a document and are using the Essentials workspace, you have several panels **docked** at the side of your screen (Mac) or application frame (PC). Docking the panels is a good option if you're working on a very small screen or just want to keep everything obsessively tidy.

To open a docked panel, just single-click on its name.

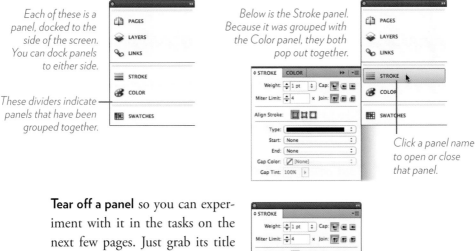

Each of these is a panel, docked to the side of the screen. You can dock panels to either side.

These dividers indicate panels that have been grouped together.

Below is the Stroke panel. Because it was grouped with the Color panel, they both pop out together.

Click a panel name to open or close that panel.

Tear off a panel so you can experiment with it in the tasks on the next few pages. Just grab its title tab, drag it off to the side, and drop it on the window. It looks like this:

To dock a panel to the side, grab it by its title tab and drag it toward the edge. When it gets within a few pixels, the panel snaps to the edge. You can dock an open panel, like the Stroke panel above, or collapse it as shown on the opposite page and then dock it.

TASK 3 Play with a typical panel

Use the Stroke panel shown on the opposite page, or open another, such as the Character panel, which you can **open from the Type menu.** Read each of the captions below and follow their directions until you can click on something and *know what to expect.*

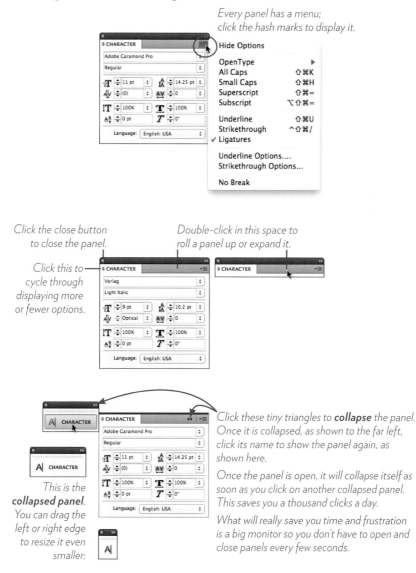

Every panel has a menu; click the hash marks to display it.

Click the close button to close the panel.

Double-click in this space to roll a panel up or expand it.

Click this to cycle through displaying more or fewer options.

*Click these tiny triangles to **collapse** the panel. Once it is collapsed, as shown to the far left, click its name to show the panel again, as shown here.*

Once the panel is open, it will collapse itself as soon as you click on another collapsed panel. This saves you a thousand clicks a day.

*This is the **collapsed panel**. You can drag the left or right edge to resize it even smaller:*

What will really save you time and frustration is a big monitor so you don't have to open and close panels every few seconds.

TASK 4 Group and ungroup panels

Panels can be grouped together to save space on your screen. You can move the group around, collapse it, dock it, etc. When a panel is grouped, you have to click on its tab bar (or double-click in the empty space to the right of the tab) to see the panel.

This is a collapsed group. Work with it as explained on the previous page.

This is a group of panels I use frequently, but not often enough to keep them stacked on my screen.

The trick to grouping a panel is to make sure when you drag it into the collection, *the blue bar appears around the entire group,* as shown below, and not just a blue bar at the top or the bottom. **To ungroup,** drag a title tab away and drop it on the window.

Drag the top part of any panel into the top part of any other panel. Watch for this blue border around the entire panel! When you see the blue border, let go.

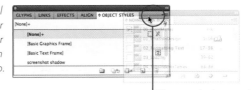

This panel is being added to an existing group.

TASK 5 Stack and unstack panels

If you have room on your screen to keep your most-used panels open and available, stack them. **To stack panels,** drag one on top of another. When you see a blue bar across the top, bottom, or either side (whichever end you want the panel to stack onto), let go, as shown on the top of the opposite page. **To unstack a panel,** drag its title tab away and drop it on the window.

The Transform panel is being stacked at the bottom of the Swatches panel. You can stack a panel on top of another, beneath another, insert it between two other stacked panels, or attach them at the sides.

Notice the blue bar—this is your visual clue that you've connected the two.

This is the stack. Drag the top bar to move the whole stack.

The Control panel

The Control panel is that area across the top of your window, just below the menu commands. *Options in the Control panel change depending on what is selected in the document.* For instance, if your insertion point is flashing in text, you'll see text options in the Control panel; if you use the *black* Selection Tool to select a graphic object, you'll see different options for manipulating the graphic.

This means that you should not try looking for an option or specification in the Control panel until *after* you have selected the item you want to affect!

There is an overwhelming collection of tiny little icons in the Control panel. Keep checking the **tool tips,** as shown below (**hover** over an icon and the tool tip appears). As you learn InDesign, more and more of the icon buttons will become useful to you in your daily creativity.

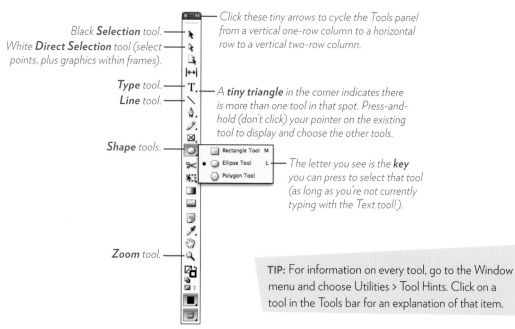

This is what the Control panel looks like when a shape is selected.

By the way, this is a hugely useful button; see pages 150, 151, 155.

The Tools panel

The Tools panel might be familiar to you from other applications. In InDesign, you can change its shape and move it, but you can't add or delete tools from it. The Tools panel, like the Control panel, cannot be grouped, stacked, nor docked on the side.

If the Tools panel is not showing, choose it from the Window menu.

Click these tiny arrows to cycle the Tools panel from a vertical one-row column to a horizontal row to a vertical two-row column.

Black **Selection** tool.

White **Direct Selection** tool (select points, plus graphics within frames).

Type tool.
Line tool.

*A **tiny triangle** in the corner indicates there is more than one tool in that spot. Press-and-hold (don't click) your pointer on the existing tool to display and choose the other tools.*

Shape tools.

	Rectangle Tool	M
●	Ellipse Tool	L
	Polygon Tool	

*The letter you see is the **key** you can press to select that tool (as long as you're not currently typing with the Text tool!).*

Zoom tool.

TIP: For information on every tool, go to the Window menu and choose Utilities > Tool Hints. Click on a tool in the Tools bar for an explanation of that item.

Hide or show the rulers

You will be using the **rulers** constantly for pulling out guides and for setting measurements in formatting fields. Whichever measurement system the ruler displays becomes the measurement system in the panels and dialog boxes. Mostly, you will be changing the rulers back and forth between inches and picas (see page 20 about picas)—maybe you don't think so yet, but trust me, you will. So learn this nifty shortcut for changing the measurement now.

TASK 6 Change the ruler settings

1   If the rulers aren't showing: From the View menu, choose "Show Rulers."

2   Right-click on the horizontal ruler across the top of the window or the vertical ruler down the side.

3   In the contextual menu that appears, choose a measurement increment. (For the future, also note the other options in this contextual menu!)

TASK 7 Using ruler guides on the page

1   Make sure the rulers are showing, as in Step 1, above.

2   Simply press the cursor in the ruler and drag onto the page.

3   **To move a ruler guide,** get the black Selection tool, press on it and drag it.

4   **To remove guides,** get the black Selection tool, click on a guide, then hit Delete or Backspace. Also, see the options in "Grids & Guides" from the View menu—you can **hide the guides, lock them, and delete all at once.**

5   When **"Snap to Guides"** is turned on (from the "Grids & Guides" options mentioned in Step 6), objects will jump to the nearest guide when you drag close to it. It's kind of freaky because you can actually feel the guide pull the graphic to it and then bump into it.

6   **To create a horizontal guide while dragging a vertical one,** or to create a vertical guide while dragging a horizontal one, hold down the Option key (PC: Alt key) while dragging.

7   **To create a guide across a double-page spread,** hold down the Command key (PC: Control key) and drag the ruler.

8   **To set the same guides on all the pages of a document,** put them on the Master Pages; see pages 14–15.

Create and hide or show the guides

If you didn't change the default settings when you created your page at the beginning of this chapter, you should see margin guidelines a half inch from the edges of the page. These guides do not print, *nor do they prevent you from doing anything*—they are there only to show you the margins you set up when you created the document. They are for you to design around.

The menu command to hide, show, and lock the guides is in the View menu, under "Grids & Guides." Learn the keyboard shortcut to hide and show the guides because you will be constantly turning them off and on.

Smart Guides

Smart Guides appear automatically to help you line things up. If they're turned on, you'll see **green guides** showing up all the time. They can show you when an element is placed the same distance between another element, when frame edges are aligned, when centers of items are aligned, and more.

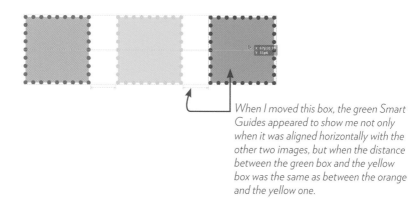

When I moved this box, the green Smart Guides appeared to show me not only when it was aligned horizontally with the other two images, but when the distance between the green box and the yellow box was the same as between the orange and the yellow one.

Smart Guides are very handy, but they sometimes make it difficult to place a guideline or an element in an exact position because the Smart Guides want to take over. So if you have trouble with a guide or item jerking away from the place where you want to put it, turn off Smart Guides (View > Grids & Guides). Learn the keyboard shortcut so you can do it instantly whenever you want.

> **TIP:** If you hit the Tab key (*not* while you're typing), **all the panels and the rulers disappear** so all that's left is the window. This is a great way to remove all the clutter so you can see your page. This also might happen accidentally, so don't freak out—just tap the Tab key again to bring everything back.

Know your defaults

As you type in InDesign or create shapes, the text appears with a font and size and color, and shapes appear with a stroke (a border) and a fill inside the shape. They automatically appear with whatever has been set as the **defaults,** and then you change the text or the shape to what you want.

But that wastes a lot of time, changing things every time you create them. So it's really important to set your own defaults. It's this easy: Choose what you want to see *before* you create it.

That is, if you plan to create a lot of type in 11-point purple Garamond text, then **first make sure nothing is selected.** Either get the black Selection tool and click on an empty space, *or* go to the Edit menu and choose "Deselect All" (learn the keyboard shortcut so you can do it quickly whenever you want).

Now, **while nothing is selected,** choose 11-point Garamond text and the color purple from the menus or the panels.

Now when you type (as explained in Chapter 2), it will always be in 11-point Garamond purple *until* you change the defaults again.

Keep this in mind as you work in InDesign.

If you want to draw seven circles, all with a blue fill (the inside color) and a dotted line stroke (the border) that is 5 points wide, **first make sure nothing is selected,** then choose those specifications, and *then* get the Ellipse tool and draw your seven circles.

This will create defaults for the document that you are working in.

But you can also **create application defaults for all documents** that you open from here on out. Just open InDesign, but *do not* open a document. Now choose what you want from the menus and the Preferences (Preferences are in the InDesign menu). Anything you can choose from a menu or the Preferences pane becomes the default for every new document you open.

This might not seem so important right now, but keep it in mind. The day will come when you'll say, "Aha! I want to set *this* as an application default!" And you will know exactly what to do.

All sorts of visual clues

Over the years you have become accustomed to noticing the tiny changes in a cursor or items on the page (like red dots under text) that give you clues about what is going on. Heighten that awareness while working in InDesign.

The cursors change constantly while you're using them—the black Selection tool cursor changes when it's near the corner of a frame or on a handle or inside a selected object, etc. The Eyedropper tool flips back and forth, the white Selection tool adds tiny symbols to itself, and more. Every cursor change indicates something that tool can do specifically because it is in that position (hovering over a handle, for instance). Throughout the book I will call your attention to them, but there's not room to mention them all! Keep a lookout. Be conscious.

Tool tips abound. Hover any tool over fields and icons in the panel, and a tool tip appears to tell you what that item is for. This is hugely useful.

*Hover the tip of your pointer over any item in a panel to display the **tool tip** that tells you what that item does.*

Every graphic and every piece of text is contained within a frame. Every frame has eight handles (one on each corner and each side), plus several other gadgets, as shown below. When a cursor is positioned on one of these handles or gadgets, it changes to give you a visual clue that tells you something will happen if you were to press-and-drag. Watch for these!

*This is the **Anchored Object** control, which lets you attach any frame to a text frame so it flows along with the text—drag this into text. When anchored, this square becomes an anchor (see page 219); delete the anchor to unattach the frame from the text.*

*When the Selection tool cursor is near a corner, it turns into a **curved arrow**; if you drag at that point, it rotates the frame.*

*This is the **Live Corners** control, which allows you to adjust the corners. See page 139.*

*Notice the donut in the middle of the frame. This is the **Content Grabber**; you can tell because the cursor has turned into a grabber hand. See page 146.*

I suggest you turn off some of these gadgets (hide them) until you need to use them; if you don't, weird things happen that you won't know how to fix. **To turn them off,** from the View menu, choose "Extras" and hide the items.

Master pages

When you create a document with more than one page, typically there are items you want to put on all the pages, such as page numbers, or perhaps a header or a logo. Every document has "Master Pages" built into it, which is where you put items that you want to appear on every page. At any point, you can override any item to remove it from a particular page, so don't think you are stuck with whatever you put there.

There is lots you can do with master pages, so I hope this introduction will lead you to discovering more. Check out the panel options and the Help files.

TASK 8 Set up a document and use master pages

1 Create a new document, and in the "New Document" dialog (as shown on page 4), make it 8 pages, letter sized, portrait, and make sure to check the box for "Facing Pages."

2 When "Facing Pages" is checked, the "Margins" change so you can set a different inside margin from the outside, as shown below. Typically the margin on the inside is larger to allow for the binding on that edge, whether it be a book or a stapled booklet or a bound report.

   To set different measurements for the various margins, click the lock icon so it turns into a broken lock icon, as shown.

   If the measurement system is something you don't know what to do with, such as points and picas, you can enter a number in inches—just type the letter i after the number of inches. For instance, enter .75i if you want a three-quarter–inch margin. InDesign will automatically translate it into the current measurement system (see page 10).

When using facing pages, you can set the inside margin separately from the outside.

3 You can change the settings at any time; for now, click OK.

4 Your document opens and you only see one page, even though you chose facing pages! That's because odd-numbered pages, such as page 1, are always on the right-hand side. Think of a book—the first page is a single page, then you turn the page and you see the double-page spread, the facing pages (they face each other).

   So turn the page of your document: Choose a page from the page field in the bottom-left corner of the window, *or* open the Pages panel from the Window menu and double-click the page numbers.

To go to the
master pages,
double-click here.

Explore the options in the
panel menu.

Double-click a page icon to
center that **page** on the screen.
Double-click the page numbers
to center the **spread** on the screen.

Important: When choosing actions from the
panel menu, **the action applies to the page
that is selected in the panel window,** not to
the page you are looking at on the screen!

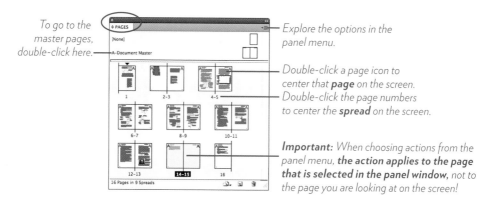

5   **Go to the master page spread:** Choose "A-Document Master" from
    the page menu in the bottom-left corner of the window, *or* double-
    click on the master page icon in the Pages panel, as shown above.

6   On this master page spread, you can draw or place any **graphic** on
    these pages that you want to appear on all pages in the document.

    You can drag in **guidelines** for placement, as explained on page 10.

    You can change the **margins** and add **columns:** From the Layout
    menu, choose "Margins and Columns...."

    You can create **text frames** for headers and footers (see Chapter 2
    about text frames). **To create automatic page numbers:**

        Get the Type tool. Press-and-drag diagonally downward to the right
        to create a small text frame. From the Type menu, choose "Insert
        Special Character," then "Markers," then "Current Page Number."

        Now get the black Selection tool. Hold down the Option key
        (PC: Alt key), and with the Selection tool, press-and-drag that text
        frame to the opposite page.

7   Go to your *document* page, as described in the callout above (double-
    click a page icon in the Pages panel). Flip through the pages on the
    screen and you'll see that they are automatically numbered, and any
    margins or columns you added are shown on every page. Notice that
    on *document* pages, you cannot select anything that was placed on a
    master page. You can, however, "Hide Master Items" from the panel
    menu. If you choose to "Override All Master Page Items," you can
    select individual master items, then move, change, or delete them.

If everything goes goofy

If you or someone else has been playing with defaults and now every time you try to do something, goofy things happen, you might want to reset all the defaults back to the factory settings and start over.

TASK 9   Reset all defaults

1   Quit InDesign, if it's open.

2   Hold down all these keys:

Mac: Shift Option Command Control

PC: Shift Ctrl Alt

3   With those keys held down, open InDesign.

4   When you see the message asking if you want to delete the preference files, click "Yes."

Try this!

Discover how to zoom in and out of your page (check the View menu). Practice doing it and using the keyboard shortcuts until you can resize the page easily. InDesign zooms in on whatever is selected on the page.

Also **experiment** with the Zoom tool from the Tools panel—press-and-drag with the tool to zoom into exactly the spot you want. Then use the keyboard shortcut to fit the page back into the window.

Set up the **panels** you think you will want to use—stack them and dock them and group them as you like. Make a **workspace**, as explained on page 5, and give it your name so you can choose it whenever you want. Experiment with **changing the workspaces:** Choose various setups from the Window > Workspace menu. Then carry on to the next chapter!

TIP: Best keyboard shortcut: While working in InDesign, use the **W** key to see a preview of your page without all the ruler guides, frame guides, etc. Hit **W** again to show everything. (The only trick is that you can't use this shortcut if you're typing!) You can also click the *Preview* icon at the bottom of the Tools panel to hide and show the preview.

SECTION II

designing with **TEXT**

Graphic design is about text. If there is no text on the page, it's not graphic design— it's art. The secret to professional-looking graphic design is knowing how to format that text. Not just choosing a font and making it bold or italic, but knowing how to space the text properly, use tabs and indents, organize information with tables, etc.

And part of working professionally is working efficiently, so in this section you'll learn how to use style sheets and how to take advantage of the defaults so you don't waste time changing your formatting constantly.

So although this isn't the sexiest section, knowing all these things will make the difference between mediocre graphic design and masterful graphic design.

The modern typographer

must have the capacity

for taking great pains

with seemingly

unimportant detail.

To her, one typographic point

must be as important

as one inch,

and she must

harden her heart

against the accusation

of being too fussy.

Hans Schmoller, typographer, 1916–1985

2 Text Frames & Formatting

One of the most important things to learn in InDesign is how to control the text frames, which is completely different from anything you've experienced in a word processor. It's very empowering. Being able to pick up the text in a neat little package and move it and set it down anywhere you want—amazing. Roll it up, widen the columns, thread the copy throughout the pages, separate headlines from the body, choose background colors—oh the things you can do.

And since graphic design is mostly text, knowing how to control your text frames is also a really *important* feature.

Get used to points and picas

When working with text, you really need to get used to working with **points and picas.** You're already familiar and comfortable with point sizes of type because you've been choosing font sizes for years in all your other applications. So you have a pretty good idea of how big 12 points is, and 12 points is one pica. There are 6 picas in one inch. Which of course makes 72 points per inch. And that's all there is to it.

12 points	=	1 pica	*A measurement is written as, for example, **6p3** or **39p0**.*
6 picas	=	1 inch	*The number before the **p** is **picas**, and the number after the*
72 points	=	1 inch	***p** is **points**. It's just like writing "6 ft.3" for 6 feet and 3 inches.*

The reason it's better to use a measuring system of points and picas when working with type is because the incremental units are small and thus easier to work with. You might want to add *half* of a point to the leading value (the space between the lines), or use a type size of 10.3 because 10 point is just too small and 10.5 is a wee bit too large for that particular project. It's much easier to get an idea of how much space is between the paragraphs when you can set 6 points of space instead of .0833 inches of space.

Know how to change the rulers

You can change the rulers with the click of the mouse; when you change the rulers, all the settings in every measurement panel change as well. That is, when you change the horizontal ruler to inches, the horizontal field in the Transform panel changes as well, and so does the horizontal field in the Preferences and the Document Setup, etc.

The horizontal measurement (width) displays inches right now because I set the horizontal ruler to inches.

The vertical measurement (height) displays points and picas right now because I set the vertical ruler to picas.

To change the ruler measurement system: Right-click on one of the rulers (horizontal or vertical) and choose the increment from the menu that appears.

I regularly flip back and forth between picas and inches because it's still easier to specify a page size in inches or some boxes in inches. Generally, though, I tend to leave the rulers in picas until I need inches for something specific.

Putting text on the page

Since you've been working with a computer for a while, you already know that you need to first select the text and *then* choose the formatting.* So all you need to know here is how to do that specifically in InDesign. You're also accustomed to using a toolbar or a panel to change formatting, so all you need to know is where those are. (Both of these things are explained in Chapter 1).

But first, you need to know how to put text on the page. Putting text on a page in InDesign is completely different from doing it in a word processor or an email message. (If you're accustomed to using text in Illustrator or Photoshop, it will seem a little more familiar.)

Every piece of text in InDesign is inside a **text frame.** This frame is movable; that is, you can pick it up and move it anywhere you want. You can resize it, reshape it, rotate it, fill it with color, put a shadow on it, put it in front or behind other objects. You can break the text frame into many individual frames and connect them all together so the story flows continuously through the individual pieces.

The following task walks you through the process of creating a text frame, typing into it, and then manipulating the frame. What you learn here will apply to every project you ever create in InDesign.

TASK 1 Create a text frame and type into it

You can import text from any word processor (see page 29), but often you will type directly on the page.

1 Get the Type tool from the Tools panel.

2 Create a text frame in which to type:
   With the Type tool, *press* (don't click) on an empty area of the page and drag diagonally downward to the right to create a rectangular frame several inches wide and a couple inches deep, then let go.

3 As soon as you let go of the mouse, the insertion point starts flashing in the upper-left corner of the text frame, signaling that you can start typing. (It doesn't matter at this point where the cursor is.)

   Before you start typing, read the information on the following page about frame edges.

—*continued*

*Just as in any application, when the insertion point is flashing you can **change the formatting specs** and what you type next will be in that formatting. For instance, if your next word is to be italic, use the keyboard shortcut to choose italic, then type. When finished with the italic text, hit the same keyboard shortcut again to toggle *off* italic. Try it!

A note on text frames and edges: Now, whether or not you actually *see* the rectangular text frame when you let go of the mouse depends on whether the "Frame Edges" are showing or not (turn them on or off as described below). If they are showing, you'll see a frame edge with the insertion point flashing, as shown below-left; if they are not, you will still see the insertion point flashing, but the frame will be invisible, as shown below-right.

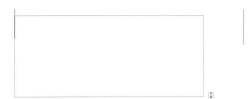

You can type into either one, and whether you choose to show the frame edges or not depends on how you like to work. For now, it's probably a good idea to see them so you understand what's happening on your page. At any time you can turn them off so you can see the page design better. Learn the keyboard shortcut so you can flip them on and off easily.

To show or hide frame edges, go to the View menu, to "Extras," and choose "Show Frame Edges" so they are visible, or "Hide Frame Edges" so they disappear. Try it.

4 Your insertion point should still be flashing in the upper-left corner of the frame.* Type into the text frame.

The text will use the font, size, and color that has been set as a default. (Remember what you learned about defaults and how to control them on page 12, but for now, just type.)

As you type, the text bumps into the right edge and automatically wraps back to the left edge (so do *not* hit a Return or Enter key at the ends of the lines!). Type several lines, until the text stops appearing in the frame and you see a red plus sign, as shown below.

Know that when all words are said and a man is fighting mad, something drops from eyes long blind, he completes his partial mind, for an instant stands at ease, laughs aloud, his

William Butler Yeats

---

*If there are any type **settings you weren't aware of,** such as a centered alignment or an indent, the insertion point won't be flashing in the upper-left corner. That's okay. Type anyway, or see page 35 about defaults.

5   Now that you've got a text frame, let's look carefully at it. You are going to work with thousands of text frames, so it's best you really understand them. And the first thing to understand is this:

The Type tool **directly affects the** individual characters. To enter text into a frame or edit existing text in a frame, use the Type tool.

The black Selection tool **treats the frame as an** object. To move, resize, or colorize a frame, use the black Selection tool.

The white Direct Selection tool **manipulates the individual points on the object (points, not handles).** To alter a frame's shape, use the white Direct Selection tool.

We want to see the frame as an **object** right now, so get the black Selection tool and single-click on the frame. You will see something like this:

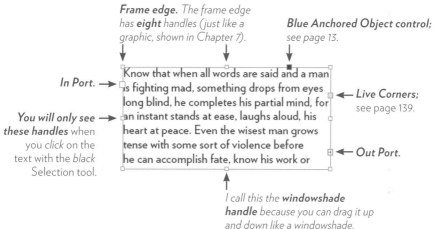

Frame edge. The frame edge has **eight** handles (just like a graphic, shown in Chapter 7).

Blue Anchored Object control; see page 13.

In Port.

You will only see **these handles** when you *click* on the text with the *black* Selection tool.

Know that when all words are said and a man is fighting mad, something drops from eyes long blind, he completes his partial mind, for an instant stands at ease, laughs aloud, his heart at peace. Even the wisest man grows tense with some sort of violence before he can accomplish fate, know his work or

Live Corners; see page 139.

Out Port.

I call this the **windowshade handle** *because you can drag it up and down like a windowshade.*

6   I recommend that you turn off things you don't need right now, such as the yellow Live Corners control (which lets you change the shape of the corners) and the blue Anchored Object control (which lets you anchor a text frame or graphic to other text, which is great, but you end up doing it accidentally all the time, which is *really* annoying and frustrating to fix). If you see the yellow and blue boxes on your frame, hide them (if you don't see them, they're already hidden):

From the View menu, choose "Extras," and then choose to hide each of those items.

Now let's go play with the text frames.

—continued

TIP: If you're using one of the Selection tools (black or white), double-click in a text frame to **switch to the Type tool automatically.**

7 **Resize the text frame:**

Get the black Selection tool and drag any side handle or corner handle. Do **not** click in an In or Out Port for now! If you accidentally do so, your cursor loads up with text—single-click on the black Selection tool in the Tools panel to let it go.

Notice as you resize the frame, the **Out Port** either displays a **red + sign**, or it's **empty.**

A **red + sign** indicates there is more text in the **frame** that has not been placed on the page; this is called *overset text.*

An **empty** Out Port means all the text in that **story** has been placed on a page.

Practice resizing the frame until you feel comfortable doing so.

In Port. → Know that when all words are said and a man is fighting mad, something drops from eyes long blind, he completes his partial mind, for *Handle.* → an instant stands at ease, laughs aloud, his heart at peace. Even the wisest man grows tense with some sort of violence before he can accomplish fate, know his work or

With the black Selection tool, drag any handle to resize the frame. Watch the text reflow.

Keep an eye on the Out Port as you resize.

Threaded text frames

Often you will work with individual text frames, but just as often you will work with longer text that needs to be broken up into several frames. Because it's something you will do millions of times, spend a couple of minutes now so you clearly understand the process.

TASK 2   Create a long story and break it into frames

1 With the Type tool, create a text frame that is about 3 inches wide and about 7 or 8 inches deep.

2 While the insertion point is flashing in that frame, go to the Control panel across the top of the window and choose 10-point type and "Auto" leading (see page 30 if you don't know how to do that).

3 Go to the Type menu and choose, "Fill with Placeholder Text." Your entire frame should now be filled with 10-point mumbo jumbo. That's good.

4 With the black Selection tool, single-click on the frame and you see that the Out Port is empty. What you have is one complete **story,** and at the moment the entire story is in one **frame.**

The concept of a *story* is important: A story might be totally contained in one frame, or it might be threaded through dozens of frames or an entire chapter. You can always tell when you've reached the end of a story because the Out Port is empty.

5   We're going to separate the story you created into several frames, and the text is going to "thread" from one frame to the next.

With the black Selection tool, roll up the text frame so it's only about two inches deep. Notice that the red plus sign appears.

6   With the black Selection tool, single-click in the Out Port. The cursor gets loaded with the rest of the text from that frame, shown below-left.

7   With that loaded cursor, press-and-drag a frame about the same size as the first one, as shown below-right. Let go, and text fills the frame.

Click on the red plus sign in the Out Port and your cursor loads up the text in the rest of the frame.

Press-and-drag that loaded cursor to create another frame. If your Smart Guides are on (see page 11), you'll see green guides when the frame size you're drawing matches the one it is next to.

8   Continue loading the cursor from the red plus sign and creating new frames with it. You'll know when all the text is placed when the frame has an empty Out Port.

Luptatae verum re, sit ut latur modic temo odisin es eost que aut estet mintiorro maxim simporitest quiatur, sandes volenihiciis expe iligenditi te parum quibus est, arum, nectibus quos vendaeres exceati aceprat iusapernate volupta tentibus vendundios pra necae nullam aborpore et, nam aut quisque nes in pore odi cusandae dolupta disqui dempore doluptate re core sam, offictatur, eatur, sent eium quas dellatio excersp ellorec eribus voloruptatur millabo. Itae nullatusant, odio. Consequi simil illique doluptatiis sequos ma voluptatur re, ullaut perestior aceped milite nos sam re paris siminimo od que nim quia debis nobitior sam voluptaspit anderumenis accat endelec uptatum faccuptatem que sit ium que perum quianto id ma plit venis invel eiciis quam, volor aut omniet derum arciiscius ipisseq uibus, consecu lparchicto con core consequi idiciet hitio is suntores denescia ium renda con nonem hiliassequi dem. Sed maximus por si audaerumque ped ut hillanti volenessit aceraes de venis quasit ommolo ium iur? Ime consecepere pro te enem quideru ptibus rent est, versped quia etureheniat.

Igenihicit, erendan dignihi llector rorem. Oluptiur?

Ferspelis escerturiore, optis ad que a nonserumqui quis est venimagnatur aciendi piendus et aut asi iur, omninus eossunt illorrum sitiati ut eate que consect aecati volores dolorion et maion reseque aut que

This is the original story. Notice that both of its ports are empty.

Luptatae verum re, sit ut latur modic temo odisin es eost que aut estet mintiorro maxim simporitest quiatur sandes volenihiciis expe iligenditi te parum quibus est, arum, nectibus quos vendaeres exceati aceprat iusapernate volupta nullatusant, odio. Consequi simil illique doluptatiis sequos ma voluptatur re, ullaut perestior aceped milite nos sam re paris siminimo od que nim quia debis nobitior sam voluptaspit anderumenis accat endelec uptatum faccuptatem que si audaerumque ped ut hillanti volenessit aceraes de venis quasit ommolo ium iur? Ime consecepere pro te enem quideru ptibus rent est, versped quia etureheniat.

Igenihicit, erendan dignihi llecto rorem.

tentibus vendundios pra necae nullam aborpore et, nam aut quisque nes in pore odi cusandae dolupta disqui dempore doluptate re core sam, offictatur, eatur, sent eium quas dellatio excersp ellorec eribus voloruptatur millabo. Itae sit ium que perum quianto id ma plit venis invel eiciis quam, volor aut omniet derum arciiscius ipisseq uibus, consecu lparchicto con consequi idiciet hitio is suntores denescia ium renda con nonem hiliassequi dem. Sed maximus por Ferspelis escerturfore, optis ad que ea nonserumqui quis est venimagnatur aciendi piendus et aut asi iur, omninus eossunt illorrum sitiati ut eate que consect aecati volores dolorion et maion reseque aut que

To see exactly how the text threads, go to the View menu, to "Extras," and check "Show Text Threads."

This is the same story broken into several text frames.
Notice: *The In Port at the beginning of the story is empty—that's your visual clue that this is where the story begins. The other In and Out Ports have **blue triangles** in them, indicating that the text threads to another frame. The last Out Port is empty, which is your visual clue that the story ends here.*

Frames are holographic!

Threaded frames don't have to be on the same page—they can be spread throughout the entire document, even hundreds of pages away. When you have the cursor loaded with the text, you can continue to turn pages, zoom in and out, move to another part of the page, and even create new pages, all while the cursor is loaded with text waiting to be placed.

To cancel a loaded cursor, click any tool in the Tools panel. *No text gets lost.* In fact, you'll discover that it's actually difficult to get rid of the text. It is always *all* contained within any remaining frame (kind of like a hologram in that you can cut a hologram into a dozen pieces, and each piece retains the entire image). You can cut the text directly with the *Type* tool, but while using the black *Selection* tool, you can't destroy any text until you delete every existing frame of the entire story.

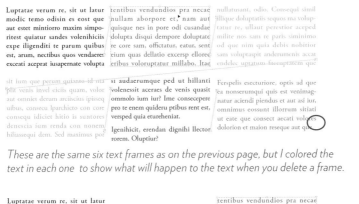

These are the same six text frames as on the previous page, but I colored the text in each one to show what will happen to the text when you delete a frame.

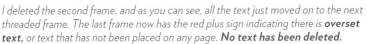

*I deleted the second frame, and as you can see, all the text just moved on to the next threaded frame. The last frame now has the red plus sign indicating there is **overset text**, or text that has not been placed on any page. **No text has been deleted**.*

TIP: You can also click the empty In Port and then create a new frame. The *beginning* of the text will flow into that new frame.

TASK 3 Experiment with those frames

Use the frames you created in Task 2 to do the following exercises.

1 **Rearrange the frames** on the page: With the black Selection tool, press-and-drag a frame or selected frames.

2 **Delete a frame or two:** With the black Selection tool, click on a frame or select more than one, then hit the Delete or Backspace key.

3 **Make more frames:** With the black Selection tool, click in either the In Port or the Out Port of any frame; this loads the cursor. Either click somewhere to automatically create a frame the width of a column on the page, *or* press-and-drag to draw a frame. Click an In Port as opposed to an Out Port, place the text, and see what happens.

TASK 4 Break the thread

In this task you're going to break the thread between the frames and put all the text back into one frame.

1 If your frame edges are hiding, show them now so you can be very clear on what is happening: From the View menu, choose "Extras," then choose "Show Frame Edges." Every frame should now display a thin blue border.

2 Find the first frame in the story (it's the only frame with an empty In Port). If you have lots of frames, make sure you've got the black Selection tool, then press Command A (PC: Control A) to select all the frames so you can see their ports.

3 With the black Selection tool, single-click on the first frame to select it.

4 Now with the black Selection tool, **double-click** on the blue triangle in the Out Port. Bingo! All the other frames are blank because *when you break the thread from one frame, it breaks it from all the subsequent frames.* The Out Port in the first frame shows the overset ✚ sign.

5 With the black Selection tool, drag the windowshade handle of the first text frame (which now holds *all* the text) all the way down until the Out Port is empty.

6 Delete all the empty text frames.

> **TIP:** With the black Selection tool, click to select a frame, then hit Delete or Backspace. Now keep the Delete or Backspace key down and click on the other frames—they disappear instantly.

27

TASK 5 Break the thread between non-consecutive frames

The previous task disconnects the first frame from all other frames. But what if you want to break the thread between two other frames?

1 Using the same frame you put back together in Task 4, separate it again into at least three frames.

2 With the black Selection tool, click on the first frame (you could do this with any frame).

3 **Single-click** on the blue Out Port; this gives you a loaded text icon. When you position this loaded icon over the next frame in the thread, a broken lock symbol appears on it, as shown here.

4 With that loaded icon, click anywhere in the frame to sever the thread.

You can also click on an In Port and disconnect from the *previous* frame in the thread. While the cursor is loaded, even if it's with a lock icon, you can click or press-and-drag with it to create another linked frame.

TASK 6 Link frames that are not yet threaded

You can link frames together that are not threaded yet.

1 Create three individual text frames, each with a little text. Make sure you can tell the text in one frame from another (maybe it's a different color or a different font or size).

2 With the black Selection tool, single-click on a frame to select it.

3 Single-click in the empty In Port or Out Port (you can also click on a red overset plus sign). The cursor loads.

When you position that cursor over another unlinked frame, the loaded cursor displays a lock icon, as shown here:

4 With that loaded lock cursor, click anywhere in the frame to link those two frames together.

Of course, at any time you can paste text inside any frame and it will all flow through.

REMINDER: You can always click a loaded icon on any tool in the Tools panel to **release all the loaded text.**

Import text

Some people (I mean me) use InDesign as a word processor. But most people create lengthy text in a word processor and then import it into InDesign. Someone might give you a text file to place, or perhaps you work in an office where you are the Star Design Geek and the others write words on which you perform Formatting Magic.

When you import, or *place,* a file that was created in a word processor, it always drops into your document as a single story, even if it covers many pages.

To place a file, you'll go to the File menu and choose "Place…," find your file, then double-click on it; you get a loaded text cursor, shown below. This is the **manual text flow** cursor, with which you can:

The manual text flow cursor icon looks like lines of text.

- Click on the page and InDesign creates a text frame for you, making it the width of a column and the depth of the page margin. The red plus sign will indicate overset text.

- *Or* press-and-drag with the loaded cursor to create individual frames to put the text in, as you did in Task 2. The red plus sign will indicate overset text.

Hold down the Option key (PC: Alt key) and you get the **semiautomatic text flow** cursor:

The semi-automatic text flow cursor looks like a dotted snake.

- Click on the page and InDesign creates a text frame for you, automatically loading up the cursor with any overset text, ready for you to click and place. This is hugely helpful.

Hold down the Shift key and you get the **automatic text flow** cursor:

The auto flow cursor looks like a snake.

- Click on the page and InDesign places the entire text file. It creates as many new pages as necessary to hold the text. Amazing.

Hold down the Shift *and* Option keys (PC: Shift *and* Alt keys) and you get the **fixed-page auto flow** cursor:

The fixed-page auto flow cursor is a boring straight line.

- This is similar to the auto flow cursor, but InDesign will only fill the existing pages; that is, it won't create as many pages as necessary.

> **TIP:** You might want to **set some options on text as it is imported.** To do so, choose the file to place, then click the box to "Show Import Options" in the Place dialog box.

Formatting text

You already know how to format text—select it with the **Type tool,** then choose the font, size, color, etc. All you need to know is where to find the formatting specifications.

Character-specific formatting

Character-specific formatting is that which applies to individual characters. The characters must be highlighted with the Type tool or your formatting choices won't be applied. This kind of formatting is found in the Character panel or the *Character Formatting Controls* in the Control panel (they have the same options), as shown below.

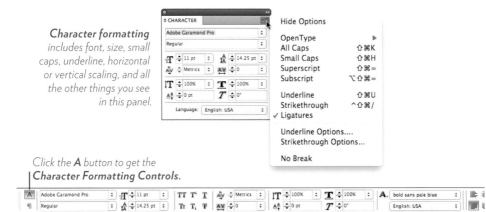

Character formatting
includes font, size, small
caps, underline, horizontal
or vertical scaling, and all
the other things you see
in this panel.

Click the **A** button to get the
Character Formatting Controls.

Everything in the Character panel is also in the Control
panel across the top of the window, easily accessible.

This text was formatted with character-specific formatting.
(See Chapter 8 for more specifics on formatting text with color.)

TIP: Although you can switch back and forth between the *Character* and *Paragraph Formatting Controls* in the Control panel, if you have a large screen, both panels actually show up at the same time—they just switch places horizontally. Check your panel.

Paragraph-specific formatting

Paragraph-specific formatting is that which applies to the entire paragraph, no matter how many characters in that paragraph are selected. In fact, you don't even need to select characters to apply any paragraph specific formatting—merely clicking the Type tool in a paragraph to set an insertion point flashing is enough to select the entire paragraph.

Paragraph formatting
includes alignment, indents and
tabs (Chapter 5), paragraph
space before and after (Chapter
3), style sheets (Chapter 6),
and everything you see listed
in the panel menu.

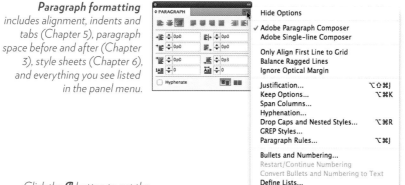

Click the ¶ button to get the
Paragraph Formatting Controls.

Most things in the Paragraph panel are also in the Control
panel across the top of the window, easily accessible.

Don't forget to
*use the **tool tips**!*

And being fap, sir, was (as they say) cashiered:
and so conclusions passed the careers.
BARDOLPH, *The Merry Wives of Windsor*, 1.1.163–164

fap: on a drinking bout; fuddled;
confused or stupefied with alcohol

Bardolph responds to Slender's charge that his purse
was stolen by Falstaff and his cohorts.

To be *cashiered* is to be dismissed
from an office or from military service in disgrace.
Slender being fap, his *conclusions*, or his judgments and
reasonings, *passed the careers*, which is to make a charge
in a jousting tournament. In other words, the matter got
out of hand, but it was Slender's own fault.

This text was
formatted with
character-specific
formatting *for the*
fonts, point sizes,
and colors, but the
spacing between
paragraphs, the
alignment, and the
style sheets are
paragraph-specific.

Character- or paragraph-specific formatting

There is one time when you can apply character or paragraph formatting without using the Type tool. You can select the entire frame or many frames with a click of the black Selection tool, and then apply any formatting you want. The formatting will apply to everything in the frame.

Formatting text frames

The text frame itself has many formatting options. You can create columns directly inside a frame, choose a border stroke and customize it, fill the frame with color or a gradient, alter the shape, and much more. This book can't cover all the possibilities, but here are some techniques to get you started. Chapter 7 on Graphics has more details about strokes and fills, and Chapter 8 on Color has all the details on creating and choosing colors.

TASK 7   Add a stroke and fill to the text frame

Every frame has a stroke (the default is "None" so you don't see it)
and a fill (also "None"), but you can change those when appropriate.

1   Create a frame with text, *or* use one of the frames you've already created.

2   With the black Selection tool, click on the frame to select it.

3   Open the Swatches panel. Click the **Container** box to make sure
the formatting changes apply to the frame, not the text.
Click the **Stroke** box (shown below), then click a color.

4   Open the Stroke panel. Choose a stroke "Type" from the pop-up menu.
Enter a "Weight" in the field, or choose from the options.

5   Go back to the Swatches panel and click on the **Fill** box (see below).
Choose a fill color, then make it a **tint** of the color: Click in the "Tint"
field and then drag the slider that appears, *or* enter a value.

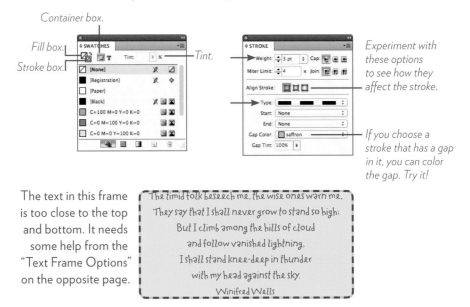

Container box.

Fill box.

Stroke box.

Tint.

Experiment with these options to see how they affect the stroke.

If you choose a stroke that has a gap in it, you can color the gap. Try it!

The text in this frame
is too close to the top
and bottom. It needs
some help from the
"Text Frame Options"
on the opposite page.

The timid folk beseech me, the wise ones warn me,
They say that I shall never grow to stand so high;
But I climb among the hills of cloud
and follow vanished lightning,
I shall stand knee-deep in thunder
with my head against the sky.
Winifred Wells

TASK 8 Use frame options to add inset spacing

The "Text Frame Options" dialog lets you set the text a certain amount of space from the edge of the frame. This easily expands your design options. Follow these steps to create something like the example below.

1 Make a text frame and put some text in it.

2 Format the text appropriately.

3 While the insertion point is in the text frame *or* when it is selected with the black Selection tool, go to the Object menu and choose "Text Frame Options…." You'll get the dialog box shown below.

Change the "Inset Spacing" and experiment with the "Vertical Justification."

Click the "Preview" button so you can see the changes.

Keep in mind that you can tell a text frame to create **columns.** *I personally don't care for the spacing issues when using this feature, but you should experiment with it.*

To set different spacing between all four edges, click the lock to unlock it. (See page 20 about using points and picas for measuring.)

This sets the text within the space vertically.

On the left, you can see the selected frame and how the text sits inside of it with an inset of 10 points.

I put a stroke type of "Thin-Thick" on the frame and changed its "Gap Color" to a pale tint.

Double double toil and trouble

MUMMY is an ancient medicine made from wrapped and dried bodies, mostly from Egypt. Paracelsus, the sixteenth-century physician, alchemist, and occultist states, "There is no remedy more certain and more fitting for the human body than the human body itself reduced to a medicament." He compares its power to that of the alchemical Philosopher's Stone. Mummy is seen in old recipes and medical books to cure a remarkable variety of illnesses, and was hugely popular among the Elizabethans—Sir Francis Bacon always carried a pouch full of it on his person. Certain kinds of mummy could reconcile estranged husbands and wives—a useful medicament for Macbeth!

The pharmaceutical firm Merck & Co. sold Egyptian mummy in their catalogs up until 1908.

Double double toil and trouble

MUMMY is an ancient medicine made from wrapped and dried bodies, mostly from Egypt. Paracelsus, the sixteenth-century physician, alchemist, and occultist states, "There is no remedy more certain and more fitting for the human body than the human body itself reduced to a medicament." He compares its power to that of the alchemical Philosopher's Stone. Mummy is seen in old recipes and medical books to cure a remarkable variety of illnesses, and was hugely popular among the Elizabethans—Sir Francis Bacon always carried a pouch full of it on his person. Certain kinds of mummy could reconcile estranged husbands and wives—a useful medicament for Macbeth!

The pharmaceutical firm Merck & Co. sold Egyptian mummy in their catalogs up until 1908.

Manipulating frames

Practice doing these tasks until you feel comfortable and know what to expect when you do it. All of the steps below require a text frame on the page.

TASK 9 Rotate a text frame

1 Get the black Selection tool.

2 Select the frame or frames you want to rotate.

3 Position the tip of the pointer near any corner point and watch for it to become a curved arrow. Press and drag.

You can also enter a value into the Transform panel, in the "Rotation Angle" field. This makes it easy to match angles of different frames.

TASK 10 Resize the text and the frame

Try this on a headline in its own frame and also on a paragraph of text.

1 Get the black Selection tool.

2 Single-click on the frame you want to resize (this selects it, of course).

3 Hold down the Command and Shift keys (PC: Control and Shift keys), then press on any handle and drag.

One Other Gaudy Night

One Other Gaudy Night

This is a quick and easy way to resize text. The field that displays the font size will give both measurements—the original point size, plus the size it is now in parentheses.

TASK 11 Reshape the frame

You might need to change the shape of a text frame to align with an object or to create a special shape for text. It's easy to do.

1 Get the white Direct Selection tool.

2 Click on an empty space somewhere to deselect the frame.
Now click on it with the white Direct Selection tool.

3 Drag any corner point to reshape.

You can add more points to use for reshaping: Get the "Add Anchor Point Tool," which is under the Pen tool (see pages 142–143 about the Pen tool). Click on the frame edge to add points. Then get the white Direct Selection tool again and drag those new points.

*I **reshaped** this text frame with the white Direct Selection tool and the Pen tools. You can also use a text wrap (see page 191), but sometimes you need the frame itself to be a different shape.*

When I heard
the learn'd
astronomer;
when the proofs,
the figures, were
ranged in columns
before me; when I was
shown the charts and the
diagrams, to add, divide, and
measure them; when I, sitting,
heard the astronomer, where he
lectured with much applause in the
lecture-room, how soon, unaccountable, I
became tired and sick, till rising and gliding out,
I wander'd off by myself, in the mystical moist night-air, and
from time to time, look'd up in perfect silence at the stars.

—Walt Whitman

Text defaults

Be conscious of the **text defaults.** Whatever options are already selected, including any style sheets in the Paragraph Styles or Character Styles panels, the font chosen, the point size, the leading value, the tabs and indents, the color swatches, the drop caps—anything at all—whatever is already selected is what will show up when you click the Type tool and start typing. That's why sometimes you start typing and things look completely crazy.

You have total control over the defaults. Whatever you choose from any menu when there is nothing selected on the page—those options become the defaults for that document. You need to get in the habit of constantly checking to see what they are, and of setting the options *before* you click the insertion point.

TASK 12 Set the text defaults

1 Make sure nothing is selected: From the Edit menu, choose "Deselect All."

2 Choose the Type tool.

3 From the Control panel or the Character panel, choose a font and a size. From the Swatches panel, choose a color.

4 Press-and-drag with the Type tool to create a text frame, then type into it. The text is formatted with the settings you just chose.

5 Create another text frame and type into it. Still has the defaults.

6 Create another text frame and type into it. Still has the defaults.

Take advantage of this! When you learn to use style sheets (Chapter 6), you can choose to set a particular style sheet as a default so you don't have to select all the formatting elements individually.

As I explained in Chapter 1, you can set defaults for just this open document, as you just did in Task 12, above. And you can set defaults for every new document that you create (see page 12).

The Glyphs panel

One of my favorite features of InDesign is the Glyphs panel. "Glyph" is an all-encompassing word that includes not only the characters of an alphabet, but all the numbers, punctuation marks, fractions, ligatures, ornaments, swashes, foreign characters, special characters, etc., that might be included in a font. The Glyphs panel is particularly important if you're using a large OpenType font, which can hold up to 16,000 glyphs—there is no way to access many of these glyphs on your keyboard. You can find some of them in the "Special Characters" panel on the Mac or the "Character Map" on a PC, but InDesign makes the process much easier and downright fun.

If you don't see the "Recently Used" bar, click this cycle icon once or twice.

This is the Glyphs panel, available from the Type menu. These are just a few of the alternate characters in this font!

Press on a tiny triangle to see alternates for that character.

Choose a font and a style from these menus, or from the Control panel or Character panel. When you click in a text frame, the Glyphs panel displays the font of the character to the left of the insertion point.

This is the font Lady Rene, using just a few of the alternate characters.

This is the font Memoir. (I'm a sucker for script faces.) Note the variant *A*s at the beginnings and ends of the names.

TASK 13 Insert a glyph into your text

1 Create a new text frame, or use one you've already got on the screen.

2 With the Type tool, click anywhere inside the frame.

3 From the Type menu, choose "Glyphs" (if it isn't already on your screen).

4 Scroll through and see the options for the font that is shown (which is the font loaded into your insertion point).
   When you see a character you want to add, such as a fraction, double-click it.

Once you have used a glyph, you'll see it in the "Recently Used" row across the top of the panel (as shown on the opposite page). When it's in that row, you can type in your paragraph, double-click a glyph from the "Recently Used" row, then continue typing in your original font. You get to skip all the steps of having to switch to another font and back again.

You can **make your own set of glyphs** for easy access to ones you need all the time.

1 Go to the panel menu in the Glyphs panel and choose, "New Glyph Set…."

2 Name it something memorable, such as "Fractions" or "Foreign Monetary Symbols." Click OK.

3 Now you can **add glyphs to that particular set:**

   Right-click on the glyph and choose "Add to Glyph Set," then choose the set you named.

   To access that set, from the panel menu choose "View Glyph Set."

   To see all the characters again, click on the "Show" menu under the Glyphs tab, and choose "Entire Font."

TIP: InDesign has *spell checking,* of course, in the Edit menu. Also check out the "Dynamic Spelling" option, which checks your spelling as you type and fixes it for you.

Try this!

Recreate the example below, using one story that you break into separate frames and format as shown; everything you see on this page you have learned to do in this chapter; page setup information you learned in Chapter 1. The text is from Wikipedia on "Holography," but feel free to use another topic.

This is a one-page document, *not* facing pages, Letter-Half, landscape/wide orientation, 3p0 margins (or .5 inch), 3 columns.

Cut the headline from the text and paste it into a separate text frame.

Format it with a heavy face.

Resize it to fit using the technique on page 34.

These dingbats are from Zapfino. In the Glyphs panel, you'll find the dingbats at the bottom of the pane.

Copy the dingbat, resize it, then rotate it.

Change the color and tint it to 10 percent.

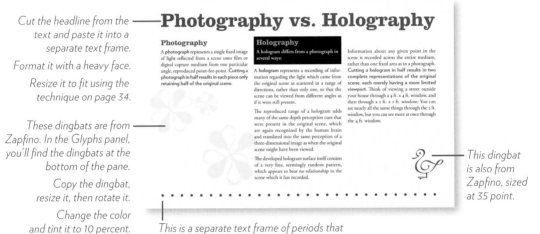

This dingbat is also from Zapfino, sized at 35 point.

This is a separate text frame of periods that I typed with spaces between, 42 point.

Here you can see all the frames and how they are threaded.

This frame has an "Inset Spacing" of 0p4, as explained on page 33, and has a fill of black. The heading is a 45 percent tint of the color so it will show up on the black background.

The heading spans all three columns.

Each dingbat is in its own text frame. You could tint each one slightly differently.

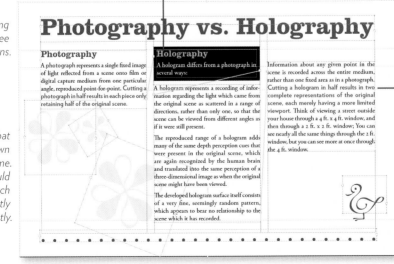

The three frames are aligned on a baseline. Use guidelines as explained in Chapter 1.

Spacing Features

You might not believe this at the moment, but knowing how to control spacing issues in InDesign is probably the most important difference between a project that looks amateurish and one that appears professional. Spacing includes the space between letters, between lines, between paragraphs, and between elements. Inappropriate or unconscious letterspacing can make type difficult to read, difficult to comprehend, and difficult to respect.

There is no formulaic method for adjusting the spacing—it is entirely dependent on the typeface, the type size, the paper, the color of ink, the purpose of the piece. The final judge is your eyes. Your eyes know if the spacing is uneven, too tight, or too loose.

Listen to your eyes.

That is, listen to your eyes—and know how to control your software.

What a difference a letter space makes

- **Kerning** is the process of adjusting the space between characters (discussed on the following seven pages).

- A good font has **auto kern pairs** built into it that make your type automatically look pretty good (see pages 42–43).

- To refine the spacing between individual characters, you can apply **manual kerning** (pages 44–45).

- To adjust a selected range of type, you can use **tracking** (see pages 46–47).

- Sometimes you might need to adjust the space between **words** (see page 48).

- You almost always need to adjust the spacing between the lines, called **leading** (see pages 49–53).

- And you must always control the spacing between **paragraphs** (see pages 54–57).

- To add specific amounts of spacing between **all the characters in a paragraph**, use the "Letter Spacing" options in the Justification dialog box (see pages 60–61).

Units of an em

An **em** (also called a *mutton*) is a typographic unit that is the width and height of the point size of the type. That is, if you're setting type in 24 point, an em is 24 points square. InDesign kerns and tracks based on *thousandths* of an em, which essentially means that it deletes or adds space based on the point size of the type. When you kern 12-point type, the unit of space added or removed is proportional; when you enlarge that 12-point type to 120 point, the kerning values are enlarged proportionally. This is a good thing.

Although it might sound like removing space equal to a few thousandths of an em is overkill, you'll be surprised at how critical it becomes as your eyes become more and more attuned to letter spacing.

REMINDER: When working with type, it's easiest to work in **points and picas**, as explained in Chapter 1 (page 20), so be sure to change at least the vertical measuring system to picas (right-click on the vertical ruler and choose "Picas").

First, set your defaults

Before we start playing with the various spacing options, let's first look at the preferences that control your kerning values. You should change these preferences while no document is open on your screen because these values will serve as the defaults for all *new* documents (existing documents will retain their own defaults). Even if you have no idea what I'm talking about, please trust me and do this:

TASK 1   Set the defaults for kerning and tracking

1   Open InDesign, if it isn't already, and make sure no document is open; close any open documents. All you should see is the menu bar across the top of your screen or window, and perhaps some panels on the right and the Toolbar on the left (or wherever).

2   From the InDesign menu, choose "Preferences…," then "Units and Increments…."

3   Change the specifications in the callout below. Type in the values you see, including the letters, such as 0.5 pt.

Click OK.

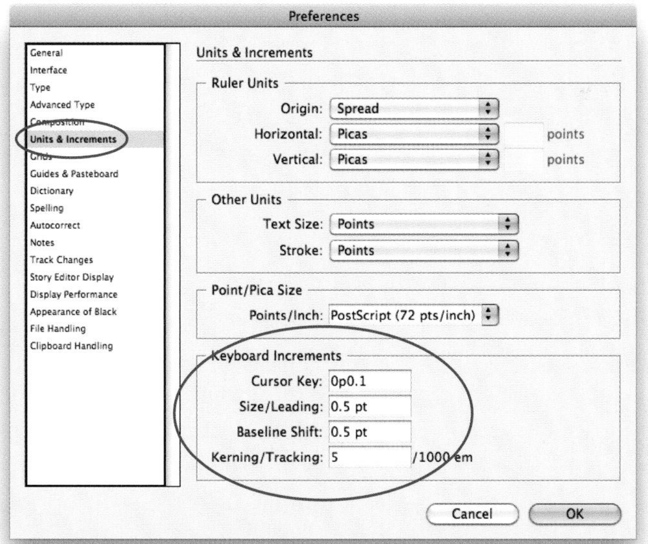

Set these increments in the units shown above. Even if your measurement system is currently in inches or something else, just type exactly what you see above and it will be okay.

These settings will allow you to adjust various elements and formatting in tiny increments.

Understand the auto kern pairs

A well-designed typeface includes a number of **auto kern pairs.** Certain pairs of letters always need kerning, such as "To" or "Va," so the letters tuck into each other nicely. The spacing happens automatically as you type, as shown here:

You can see that the spacing between the **Th** is different from that in the **To.**

The spacing is based on the auto kern pairs that the designer built into the font.

Metrics kerning

A well-designed face has the kerning built into the font **metrics** so when you type certain combinations of characters, they automatically snuggle up together. A font might have anywhere from fifty to several thousand auto kern pairs. InDesign, by default, applies these auto kern pairs, as you can tell by the Kerning field—when you select a range of text, it typically says "Metrics."

The "Metrics" in the Kerning field is your clue that InDesign is using the auto kern pairs.

The other option in this field is "Optical."

This means InDesign is using the font metrics and applying the kerning values built into the font (which is why type automatically looks better in InDesign than it does in most word processors because most word processors do not apply the auto kern pairs). However, when you click the insertion point between two characters, this same Kerning field displays a number in parentheses—that's the kerning value of the auto pair. (That number will change if you manually kern the characters, and the number will no longer be in parentheses.)

To remove the auto kern pairs (I can't think of a reason why you would do this), select the text and enter "0" (zero) in the Kerning field.

Optical kerning

If you use a typeface that does not have built-in kern pairs, that's when you want to choose the "Optical" option in the Kerning field (shown on the opposite page). Optical looks at the shapes of the letters and tries to adjust them as well as it can—without eyes.

This is a typeface designed by my daughter, Scarlett, when she was seven years old; it has no kerning pairs.

No auto kern pairs can be applied.

But you can use Optical kerning and it will do the best it can.

You'll also want to choose Optical kerning when you're using a combination of fonts, styles, or sizes because the metrics cannot apply to characters unless they are the same font, style, and size. Below is a typical case in which you would want to choose Optical kerning (you will probably need to do some manual kerning as well).

NOTE: **Kerning values always apply to the character on the left**, so if you want to apply Optical kerning, select only the characters you want to apply it to. For instance, in the example above, you would select the V *or* just click your insertion point directly after the V. If you select two characters, such as **Va**, you will also apply the Optical kerning between the **a** and the next letter to the right, which might not be what you want!

Manual kerning the space between letters

Manual kerning is when you **adjust the space between *two* characters** (that is, *two* characters as opposed to a *range* of text). This important letterspacing feature is the only one dependent on your eyes. Manual kerning is what you'll use to fine-tune your text (typically only your headline text) after all the other options have been adjusted. Manual kerning is the most important feature to master because it is a key to creating professional-level typography.

Somewhere in Time
Somewhere in Time

The most efficient way to manually kern is with the keyboard shortcuts (shown below). With each tap of the shortcut, InDesign applies the amount you have set in the preferences pane shown on page 41.

Any manual kerning you apply is *added* to the auto pair kern that might be built into the two characters. The Kerning field displays the *total amount of the auto pair kern and any manual kerning you apply.* But you don't really have to worry about the numerical value—**kerning is by eye,** not by number. So ignore all the numbers in the boxes and listen to your eyes.

Keyboard shortcuts for manual kerning: With the Type tool, single-click to set the insertion point between two characters.

	Mac	Windows
Add space:	*Option RightArrow*	*Alt RightArrow*
Delete space:	*Option LeftArrow*	*Alt LeftArrow*
x 5 increments:	*Command Option RightArrow*	*Control Alt RightArrow*
	Command Option LeftArrow	*Control Alt LeftArrow*
Delete kerning:	Select the character on the left, or select all characters, then:	
	Command Option Q	*Control Alt Q*

NOTE: The point is not to *tighten* all the spacing—the point is to make it **visually consistent** so there *appears* to be the same amount of space between all the letters.

TASK 2 Kern a word

1 Create a text frame about four inches wide, then type this word in all caps: **WATERMELON**

2 Use a sans serif font and make it 36 point.

3 Kern the word manually: With the Type tool, single-click between two characters. Use the keyboard shortcuts shown on the opposite page.

WATERMELON
WATERMELON

TASK 3 Kern a headline

1 Create a text frame about four inches wide, then type a headline into it, such as **Not for the Slow-Headed.**

2 Format the text with 36-point serif type, something like this:

Not for the Slow-Headed

3 The metrics are already applied, so now you need to manually kern it. The object is to make the spaces between letters *visually consistent.*

Not for the Slow-Headed

REMINDER: **The kerning value is applied to the character on the LEFT.** You can copy and paste that character, and the kerning value goes with it. Delete the character, and the kerning is deleted.

Tracking the space between letters

Tracking is when you **adjust the space between a selected range of characters.** Instead of applying an *individual* amount between *a pair of letters,* tracking applies the *same* amount to *all the characters that are selected.* Because tracking does not take into account the shapes of the letters, it's only useful to get a start on adjusting the space—you still need to fine-tune with manual kerning.

Any tracking you apply is *added* to the manual kerning and to the auto pair kerns. That's why you might select an entire word and apply one value of tracking, but when you click between two characters in that same word, the Kerning field displays a different value. But the Tracking value does not *affect* the Kerning value! You can manually kern between individual characters until they are visually consistent, then apply tracking and everything will tighten or loosen proportionally.

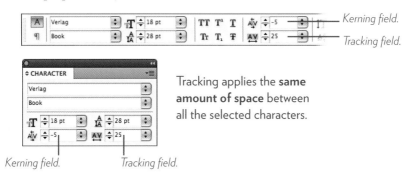

Kerning field.

Tracking field.

Tracking applies the **same amount of space** between all the selected characters.

Kerning field.   Tracking field.

Keyboard shortcuts for tracking: With the Type tool, press-and-drag over a range of characters. (These are the same shortcuts as for manual kerning.)

	Mac	Windows
Add space:	Option RightArrow	Alt RightArrow
Delete space:	Option LeftArrow	Alt LeftArrow
x5 increments:	Command Option RightArrow	Control Alt RightArrow
	Command Option LeftArrow	Control Alt LeftArrow
Delete all:	Command Option Q	Control Alt Q

TIP: You can add **tracking** to a style sheet. For instance, you might want to open up the look of the body copy— add a wee bit of tracking to a Body Copy style sheet.

TASK 4   Track a headline

1   Create a text frame about four inches wide, then type a headline into it, such as **In Pearl and Gold.**

2   Format the text with 36-point sans serif type, something like this:

In Pearl and Gold

3   The larger the type, the tighter the letterspacing it generally requires. So to get a head start on the process, you can select the entire headline and apply some tracking. If necessary, add manual kerning to finish it.

In Pearl and Gold

TASK 5   Open up the letterspacing in the body copy

1   Create a text frame about four inches wide, then fill it with text (from the Type menu, choose "Fill with Placeholder Text"). *Or* type a paragraph of text, *or* copy and paste some text.

2   Format the text: Use 10.5-point type.

3   Select all the text and apply some tracking. Just keep hitting the keyboard shortcuts to open up the spacing; see how it looks, then tighten the spacing to see how that looks. Try to get a sense of what makes the text the most readable (it's a fine line).

Herb Caen (1916–1997) of *The San Francisco Chronicle:*

It just occurred to me, with the usual thull dud, that "etaoin shrdlu" is dead. If you are under a certain age, this will mean nothing to you, more's the pity. If you are over that age, and are a printfreak besides, the mere mention of "etaoin shrdlu" may bring a tear to your peepers—the same tear that is drawn by the mere mention of such words as "running board," "25-cent martini," and, well, ok, "peepers." In the pioneer days of print journalism, the intriguing "etaoin shrdlu," pronounced roughly "Etwan Sherdlu," was the most famous and most frequent of all typographic erros. And needless to say, The Old Chronicle had more than its share.

Myriad, 7.5/9.5, -10 tracking

Herb Caen (1916–1997) of *The San Francisco Chronicle:*

It just occurred to me, with the usual thull dud, that "etaoin shrdlu" is dead. If you are under a certain age, this will mean nothing to you, more's the pity. If you are over that age, and are a printfreak besides, the mere mention of "etaoin shrdlu" may bring a tear to your peepers—the same tear that is drawn by the mere mention of such words as "running board," "25-cent martini," and, well, ok, "peepers." In the pioneer days of print journalism, the intriguing "etaoin shrdlu," pronounced roughly "Etwan Sherdlu," was the most famous and most frequent of all typographic erros. And needless to say, The Old Chronicle had more than its share.

Myriad, 7.5/9.5, 10 tracking

The space between words

Occasionally you might need to adjust the space between words. One common circumstance is with some script faces where the tails of the letters encroach on the word spaces; you might need to *tighten* the letterspacing so the characters connect to each other, but *open* the word spacing so you can read it easily.

Everyone should have a chance at an extravagant piece of folly.

Everyone should have a chance at an extravagant piece of folly.

You can also adjust the word spacing in any style sheet (see Chapter 6 on Style Sheets). For instance, if you have a font that always needs more or less word spacing and you want to use it in the headlines of your newsletter, adjust the word spacing in the headline style sheet (use the Justification dialog box, as explained on pages 60–61).

Keyboard shortcuts for word spacing: With the Type tool, press-and-drag over a range of characters.

	Mac	Windows
Add word space:	*Control Command Option *	*Control Alt *
x5 increments:	*Shift Command Option *	*Shift Control Alt *
Delete word space:	*Command Option Delete*	*Control Alt Backspace*
x5 increments:	*Shift Command Option Delete*	*Shift Control Alt Backspace*

The space between lines

It is amazing how adding a wee bit of space between the lines makes the text not only look more appealing, but easier to read. The space between lines is called **leading** (pronounced *ledding*), a name that comes from the thin strips of lead that were used for centuries to separate lines of metal type.

As with most things in life, leading has a standard from which we can deviate. The standard value for leading is 20 percent added to the point value of the type. For instance, if you use 10-point type, the standard leading value—the **Auto** leading—that InDesign applies to the text is 12 points (20 percent of 10, added to the 10, equals 12). This is written as 10/12, which means 10 point type with 12 points of leading.

When InDesign applies the standard value, the Auto leading, it is displayed in parentheses, as shown here.

But even though it's called 12-point leading, there are really only 2 extra points of space between the lines! I know, it's confusing.

The 12 points are distributed from the *baseline* (the invisible line upon which the type sits) of one line of text to the baseline of the text above.

The leading is measured from baseline to baseline.

I will be bright and
shine in pearl and gold.

The text above-right is 20/24, and it uses Auto leading, as shown here in the Control panel and the Character panel.

It's important to know these things because if you can't control your leading, it can make you crazy. So let's talk about how to control it.

Once you become conscious of linespacing, you'll start getting very fussy with it. It never ceases to amaze me what a difference even a half point of leading can do. If you have read *The Non-Designer's Design Book,* you understand how important the concept of *proximity* is to communication, and now in InDesign you will understand how to create exactly the amount of proximity you need between items for clear communication.

TASK 6 Experiment with the leading in body copy

1   Create a text frame about four inches wide, then fill it with text (from the Type menu, choose "Fill with Placeholder Text"). *Or* type a paragraph of text, *or* copy and paste some text.

2   Format the text: Select all the text and choose 10.5-point type, plus Auto leading (choose "Auto" from the Leading field pop-out menu).

3   Select all the text and change the leading values. Experiment: Take out leading, add more, add an excess, etc. Either choose an amount from the Leading menu or type in any amount. Print up a page of these paragraphs using different amounts of spacing. How do the various amounts of linespace affect the readability of the text?

You've probably noticed by now that when you choose "Auto," InDesign enters the actual amount in the field, but in parentheses.

Herb Caen (1916–1997) of *The San Francisco Chronicle:*

Every now and then, a Linotype operator would make a mistake. He would then run his finger down the two left-hand columns of the lower-case keyboard, producing the matrices "etaoin shrdlu," which filled out one line. Or, these words would be used as a guide on a galley of type, under the slug, say of "Caen." The compositor, a fellow who could read type upside down and backwards but no other way, was supposed to remove the slug and

Verlag Book, 9/10.2

Herb Caen (1916–1997) of *The San Francisco Chronicle:*

Every now and then, a Linotype operator would make a mistake. He would then run his finger down the two left-hand columns of the lower-case keyboard, producing the matrices "etaoin shrdlu," which filled out one line. Or, these words would be used as a guide on a galley of type, under the slug, say of "Caen." The compositor, a fellow who could read type upside

Verlag Book, 9/11.8

TASK 7   Play with negative leading

The leading value does not always have to be larger than the point size. In fact, the larger the font size, the less leading you need. You will regularly find yourself decreasing the leading in headlines.

1   Create a text frame and type the headline you see below.

Do not hit a Return after "Crush"—either make the text frame smaller so the line breaks at that point, *or* hit **Shift Return or Shift Enter to force a line break** (this breaks the line but does *not* create a new paragraph).

2   Notice how much unnecessary empty space is between the lines. Select all the text and reduce the leading amount. Use the keyboard shortcuts (shown below) so you can judge the appropriate amount with your eyes. You'll see the value in the Leading field change as you use the shortcut.

Vile Bezonians Crush Roman Supporters

This is 24 point type (Trade Gothic Bold) with its Auto leading value of 28.8.

Vile Bezonians Crush Roman Supporters

This is 24 point type with a fixed leading value of 23.

Keyboard shortcuts for leading: With the Type tool, press-and-drag over a range of characters. The amount of leading that is added or deleted is the amount specified in the preferences shown on page 41.

	Mac	Windows
Add leading:	*Option DownArrow*	*Alt DownArrow*
x5 increments:	*Command Option DownArrow*	*Ctrl Alt DownArrow*
Delete leading:	*Option UpArrow*	*Alt UpArrow*
x5 increments:	*Command Option UpArrow*	*Ctrl Alt UpArrow*
Auto leading:	*Shift Option Command A*	*Shift Alt Ctrl A*

Auto leading versus fixed leading

Auto leading: When the leading applied to text is *Auto* (which will be displayed in parentheses in the Control panel and Character panel, as shown on the opposite page), the space between the lines adapts as you resize the type. No matter how large or small you make the text, the leading is always proportionate to the size of the type (120 percent of the point size).

This is fine for many things. You will run into issues, however, if you enlarge the point size of any character in a line that uses Auto leading because the character with the largest amount of Auto leading takes over the whole line. It creates this kind of look:

*I*n the time of your life, live . . . so that in that wondrous time you shall not add to the *M*isery and *S*orrow of the world, but smile to the infinite delight and *M*ystery of it.

—WILLIAM SAROYAN

The Ms and the S are in a larger point size with their own Auto leading, which is greater than the Auto leading of the smaller text.

The larger characters force more space *above* the lines because the leading value goes from the baseline of the text *up* to the baseline above.

The solution is to use *fixed* leading.

Fixed leading: When you fix the leading by typing in your own value (even if it's exactly the same amount as the Auto leading value), the leading stays that value, no matter how large or small you make the text. By fixing the leading, you avoid problems like the one shown above because the line spacing will stay the same no matter what the point size of the type.

*I*n the time of your life, live . . . so that in that wondrous time you shall not add to the *M*isery and *S*orrow of the world, but smile to the infinite delight and *M*ystery of it.

—WILLIAM SAROYAN

With fixed leading, you can ensure that the space between all lines is the same.

If there are any blank characters at the end of a line (which are invisible to you!), they hold on to their leading value and can impact the line spacing. When changing the leading in a line or paragraph, make sure you select the entire line or paragraph, as shown here:

I typed the headline (the font is Pious Henry), hit a Return/Enter, and typed the byline. I plan to make the byline a smaller font size.

But when I selected the characters in the byline and reduced the font size with its Auto leading, the space between the lines did not change!

I didn't realize that there are three extra spaces at the end of the byline. If I "Show Hidden Characters" (from the Type menu), I can see them, as shown circled above.

So I selected the entire line (I triple-clicked it), and then when I changed the leading value, it affected the entire line, not just the selected characters.

The space between paragraphs

This is one of the most critical spacing features you can learn to use, in which you can add wee bits of space between paragraphs without having to hit the Enter or Return key twice. In fact, after you read this, you are never again allowed to hit Enter/Return more than once. (I'm just going to call it a Return from now on, but know that it works for the Enter or Return key.)

When you hit Return, InDesign starts a new paragraph, as you know. Automatically included in that Return is a certain amount of space between the paragraph you just finished and the new one you are starting. The default is usually 0 points or 0 inches of space, which is why one might automatically hit two Returns to make more space.

But two Returns makes a big, dorky space and all your paragraphs end up looking like disparate elements on the page. So ideally you want just about a half line between paragraphs, like what you see in this text you're reading and in the example below-right. That's where Paragraph Space After comes in.

The older Rajah was still more surprised at this. He could not think any one was really concerned about Guzra Bai, and he feared the young Rajah wished, for some reason, to quarrel with him. But he agreed to send for his wife, and messengers were at once dispatched to bring Guzra Bai to the palace.

No sooner had she come than the young Ranee began to weep, and she and the Princes gathered about their mother. Then they told the Rajah the whole story of how his mother and the nurse had sought to destroy Guzra Bai and her children, how they had been saved, and had now come to safety and great honor.

The Rajah was overcome with joy when he found that Guzra Bai was innocent. He asked her to forgive him, and this she did, and all was joy and happiness.

I hit the Return key twice at the end of each of these paragraphs. The big gaps between them separate the thoughts too much.

The older Rajah was still more surprised at this. He could not think any one was really concerned about Guzra Bai, and he feared the young Rajah wished, for some reason, to quarrel with him. But he agreed to send for his wife, and messengers were at once dispatched to bring Guzra Bai to the palace.

No sooner had she come than the young Ranee began to weep, and she and the Princes gathered about their mother. Then they told the Rajah the whole story of how his mother and the nurse had sought to destroy Guzra Bai and her children, how they had been saved, and had now come to safety and great honor.

The Rajah was overcome with joy when he found that Guzra Bai was innocent. He asked her to forgive him, and this she did, and all was joy and happiness.

Above, I set a **Paragraph Space After** of about half the type size. That is, if the point size of the type is 11 points, add about 5.5 or 6 points of space after each paragraph.

TIP: If you get confused about whether to add paragraph space **before** or **after,** just remember this guideline: **Always use Paragraph Space AFTER.** The day will come when you hit upon a design problem and discover that *there* is the perfect place to add Space Before, and then you will feel comfortable doing so. Until then, use Space After.

The amount of space between paragraphs is determined in the Paragraph panel, as shown below. Let's start with the Paragraph Space *After* because it's a little easier to understand.

The tool tips, as shown here, will appear when you hover over the icon label as a reminder of which field to use.

TASK 8   Experiment with the Paragraph Space After

In this example, you'll adjust the spacing between several paragraphs. First, **make sure your measuring system is in picas:** Right-click (or Control-click) on the vertical ruler on the left side of the window, and choose "Picas." Then:

1   Create a text frame about three inches wide and five inches deep.

2   While the insertion point is flashing in your text frame, choose 10 point for the font size.

3   Type three short paragraphs of anything. At the end of each paragraph, hit ONE Return or Enter—not two! At the moment, it might look like there is no space between the paragraphs; that's okay.

4   When you've got three paragraphs, each at least two or three lines long, select all the text.

5   In the Paragraph panel or in the Control panel with the paragraph specs showing (as shown above), enter 0p6 in the Space After field, then hit Enter. You should now see 6 points of space between each paragraph.

Experiment with other values until you can predict what will happen when you hit Enter.

TIP: Any Paragraph Space After or Before is **added onto** the leading value.

TASK 9   Combine leading and Paragraph Space After

In something like a bulleted or numbered list, you want the lines in the paragraph to be closely connected, but you want more space after each section. So tighten up the leading a wee bit, and open up the Space After.

1   Recreate the list shown below with any list of your choice.

2   Tighten the leading just a tiny bit, like half a point, and add Paragraph Space After to all paragraphs, including the headline (separately). You can immediately see the huge difference in clarity.

Rhetorical Devices

ZEUGMA: Where a word applies to two others in different senses *(John and his license expired last week)* or to two others of which it semantically suits only one *(with weeping eyes and hearts).*
ANTANACLASIS: The repetition of a word or phrase whose meaning changes in the second instance. *We must all hang together, or assuredly we shall all hang separately.*
POLYPTOTON: Repeating a word, but in a different form. *With eager feeding, food doth choke the feeder.*
ANTITHESIS: Opposition of words or phrases against each other, powerfully expressing conflict through its use of opposites. *What's past is prologue.*
CHIASMUS: A crisscross structure where a motif, phrase, idea, or grammatical structure is repeated and inverted. *I wasted Time, and now doth Time waste me.*
SYNECDOCHE: A whole is represented by naming one of its parts, or vice versa. *Take thy face hence.*
HENDIADYS: The expression of a single idea by two words connected (usually) with "and." *The dark backward and abysm of time.*

Rhetorical Devices

ZEUGMA: Where a word applies to two others in different senses *(John and his license expired last week)* or to two others of which it semantically suits only one *(with weeping eyes and hearts).*

ANTANACLASIS: The repetition of a word or phrase whose meaning changes in the second instance. *We must all hang together, or assuredly we shall all hang separately.*

POLYPTOTON: Repeating a word, but in a different form. *With eager feeding, food doth choke the feeder.*

ANTITHESIS: Opposition of words or phrases against each other, powerfully expressing conflict through its use of opposites. *What's past is prologue.*

CHIASMUS: A crisscross structure where a motif, phrase, idea, or grammatical structure is repeated and inverted. *I wasted Time, and now doth Time waste me.*

SYNECDOCHE: A whole is represented by naming one of its parts, or vice versa. *Take thy face hence.*

HENDIADYS: The expression of a single idea by two words connected (usually) with "and." *The dark backward and abysm of time.*

TASK 10 A place to use Paragraph Space Before

This example is one of the few times when it's perfect to use the Space *Before* feature instead of the Space *After*. When you have body text that is broken up with subheads, you want the subheads to be closer to the body copy it refers to and farther away from the text *above/before* the subhead. So add Space Before to subheads.

In something like a newsletter or a brochure, you'll create a style sheet (as explained in Chapter 6) for subheads to make the space appear automatically.

1 Create several short paragraphs, each with a subheading. Hit a Return after each subheading, and a Return at the end of each paragraph.

2 To each subheading, add 9 or 10 points of space to the Paragraph Space Before.

Thing Thumb Thongs! — This heading has 3 points of Space After.

This subhead has 9 points of Space Before. Thus there is a total of 12 extra points of space between the head and the subhead (plus the leading value).

Door Oil Gory Mayor
Odor oil gory mayor,
Shay ant washy oyster bay
Ant washy oyster bay,
Ant washy oyster bay!
Door oil gory mayor,
Shay ant washy oyster bay
Money lung yares a gore!

Fur Hazy Jelly Gut Furlough — Each of these subheads has Paragraph Space *Before*, which adds space *above* the paragraph/subhead. This separates each subhead from the text *above/before* it.
Fur hazy jelly gut furlough
Fur hazy jelly gut furlough
Fur hazy jelly gut furlough
Witch nor bawdy candor nigh

Hurl, Hurl, Door Gong's Oil Hair
Hurl, hurl, door gong's oil hair!
Moisten satyr knotty wart!
Moisten satyr knotty wart!
Hurl, hurl, door gong's oil hair!
Wart inhale dough way cur, nor?

Hormone Derange
O gummier hum warder buffer-lore rum
Enter dare enter envelopes ply,
Ware soiled 'em assured adage cur-itching ward
An disguise earn it clotty oil die.
Harm, hormone derange,
Warder dare enter envelopes ply,
Ware soiled 'em assured adage cur-itching ward
An disguise earn it clotty oil die.

from *Anguish Languish,* by Howard L. Chace

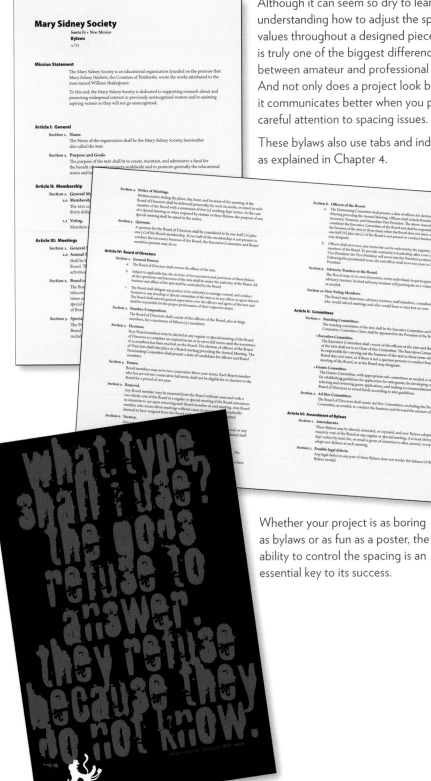

Although it can seem so dry to learn, understanding how to adjust the spacing values throughout a designed piece is truly one of the biggest differences between amateur and professional work. And not only does a project look better, it communicates better when you pay careful attention to spacing issues.

These bylaws also use tabs and indents, as explained in Chapter 4.

Whether your project is as boring as bylaws or as fun as a poster, the ability to control the spacing is an essential key to its success.

If you really have to make it fit . . .

Sometimes the text just doesn't fit and you have to cheat a little here and there to force it into the space. For instance, you might want to bring the short last word of a column up to the line above, or make a one-line statement fit on one line, or send a couple of words to the last line. Here are a few extra tricks you can use, and probably no one in the entire world will notice (which is kind of sad).

- If your text frame is flush left, widen or narrow it just a hair. Or two.

- To force one line that's just a little too long into one line, justify it.

  If that doesn't work, select the entire line and use the tracking keyboard shortcut to take out wee bits of space.

  Or do both of the above.

- If you have many pages and you want to make everything just a tiny bit shorter or a tiny bit longer, remove something like one-quarter or one-half of a point out of the leading, or add a tiny bit.

  Or select the appropriate text and use the Justification dialog box (see the following two pages) to delete/add a tiny bit of Letter Space to all of it.

- Change the Horizontal Scale of the selected characters. You can make them 2 percent wider or narrower and few people will notice. In headlines, you can get away with a little more compressing or stretching because people seem to almost expect it, which means few people will worry about it too much.

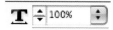 This is the Horizontal Scale field in the Control panel or the Character panel.

- Triple-click to select an entire paragraph, then use the keyboard shortcuts to track the text, adding either a tiny bit of space or deleting. This can bring the last word, an orphan, up into the paragraph, or send a couple more words down to the last line so you don't have an orphan at all.

Advanced tips: Paragraph-specific letterspacing

Feel free to skip this section—you can probably live your entire life without reading it. But if you are feeling confident about spacing issues in InDesign and want to know even more, learn about the Justification dialog box and how it impacts spacing.

First, understand that **kerning** values are "character-specific," meaning you can apply them to selected *characters.* **Tracking** values are also character-specific, but can be added to style sheets in the "Basic Character Formats" pane; when added to a style sheet, the tracking affects every character in the paragraph.

But there's another way to adjust the letterspacing in a paragraph of text, or in all headlines, a story, or an entire document—**paragraph-specific letterspacing.** Because this letterspacing does not take into consideration any tracking, kerning, or pair kern values, it is the fastest and most processor-efficient way for InDesign to adjust the space between lots of characters. This is the feature you want to use if you have pages of text to open up or tighten. (You won't see the paragraph letterspacing value reflected in the tracking or kerning fields.)

The specifications in the Justification dialog box affect all the type on the page, whether you realize it or not.

The Justification dialog box

Open the Justification dialog box in either your style sheet options or from the Paragraph panel menu. These specifications tell InDesign how much it can adjust the word spacing, the letter spacing, and even the width of characters (glyphs) when the text is justified (lined up on both the left and right sides). For instance, the defaults shown below tell InDesign that if you justify the text, it is allowed to squish the word spacing up to 75 percent to make text fit on the line, or it can expand the word spacing up to 150 percent. If necessary, it is also allowed to adjust the letter spacing where necessary, but in these specs it cannot squish or expand the letterforms/glyphs.

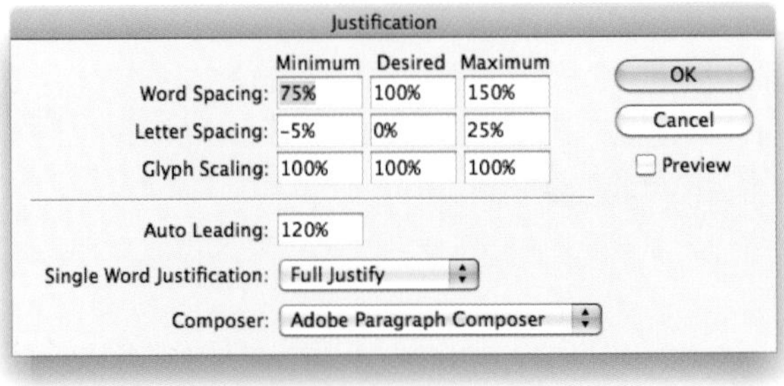

Justification			
	Minimum	Desired	Maximum
Word Spacing:	75%	100%	150%
Letter Spacing:	-5%	0%	25%
Glyph Scaling:	100%	100%	100%
Auto Leading:	120%		
Single Word Justification:	Full Justify		
Composer:	Adobe Paragraph Composer		

OK · Cancel · ☐ Preview

This is also where InDesign is told to *add* 20 percent of the point size of the type to create the Auto Leading value. You can change this if you can think of a reason to do so.

Now, there are two things to remember about these specs:

- The "Minimum" and "Maximum" amounts only apply if you **justify** the text. That is, flush right or flush left text will ignore whatever is in those fields and will simply apply the "Desired" amount.

- The "Desired" amount must be *between* (or including) the "Minimum" and "Maximum." For instance, if you want to change the "Desired" letterspacing to 30 percent, first you must change the "Maximum" to 30 percent or more.

The smaller the type size, the more letterspacing it needs, proportionally, and the larger the type, the less letterspacing it needs. So let's say you have a page of small type and you want to open up the space a little. You could do it with tracking, but it will be faster and more efficient to use the paragraph letterspacing.

So select the text or style sheet. In the Justification dialog box, first enter an amount in the Letter Spacing "Maximum" field. If your text is justified, enter the percentage that you want to increase the spacing by, and enter that same amount in the "Desired" field. If your text is *not* justified, enter any amount in the "Maximum" field, then enter your desired increase in the "Desired" field.

If you're working with large type that needs *less* letterspacing, you can enter negative numbers in the "Minimum" and "Desired" fields.

The **Word Spacing** in the Justification dialog box works the same as Letter Spacing: The designer has built into the font metrics the "spaceband," or the amount of space that appears on the page when you hit the Spacebar. You can deviate from this amount by a desired percentage. I sometimes open up the word spacing just a wee bit for clarity.

The **Glyph Scaling**, as I mentioned, can allow InDesign to squish or expand the actual letterforms to fit the text in the desired line length. Alternatively, you can use these fields for an intentionally distorted type effect! (For short pieces of text, such as the one below, you can also use the Horizontal Scale field in the Control panel or the Character panel.)

VILE BEZONIANS!

TIP: To force a **line break** without making a new paragraph, use Shift Return or Shift Enter.

Try this!

Recreate a letter like the one below. Do not hit double Returns/Enters to create the spacing! Everything can be done with Paragraph Space After and with leading. Once you have the letter set up, you can use it as a template for future letters.

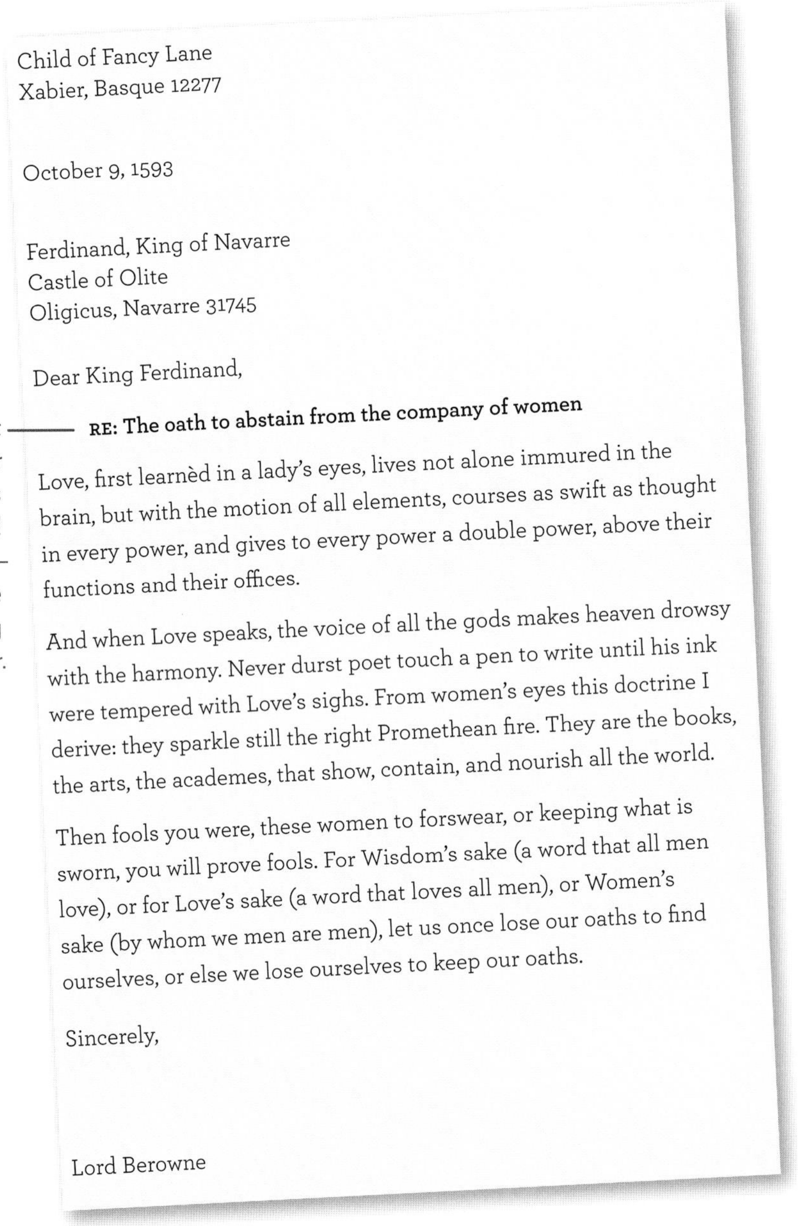

Child of Fancy Lane
Xabier, Basque 12277

October 9, 1593

Ferdinand, King of Navarre
Castle of Olite
Oligicus, Navarre 31745

Dear King Ferdinand,

I did *not* hit ——— **RE: The oath to abstain from the company of women**
the Spacebar
to move this
text over!
I used a tab—
see the
following
chapter.

Love, first learnèd in a lady's eyes, lives not alone immured in the brain, but with the motion of all elements, courses as swift as thought in every power, and gives to every power a double power, above their functions and their offices.

And when Love speaks, the voice of all the gods makes heaven drowsy with the harmony. Never durst poet touch a pen to write until his ink were tempered with Love's sighs. From women's eyes this doctrine I derive: they sparkle still the right Promethean fire. They are the books, the arts, the academes, that show, contain, and nourish all the world.

Then fools you were, these women to forswear, or keeping what is sworn, you will prove fools. For Wisdom's sake (a word that all men love), or for Love's sake (a word that loves all men), or Women's sake (by whom we men are men), let us once lose our oaths to find ourselves, or else we lose ourselves to keep our oaths.

Sincerely,

Lord Berowne

4 Tabs and Indents

I realize that most people hate tabs and indents, mainly because they don't quite understand how they work. You see, tabs and indents always do what you tell them to do! If you have trouble with tabs and indents, it is only because you don't know what you are telling them! Don't holler at those poor tabs—they are trying to do what you want; it's your responsibility to figure out how to tell them what to do. They always work. They are extremely dependable and reliable and logical (yes, logical). So this chapter teaches you how to take advantage of their dependability.

Also check out Chapter 5 about the table feature because some designers prefer to use tables rather than tabs and indents.

Things you should know about tabs and indents

You must first understand how tabs and indents behave.

A The Tabs panel is where the tabs and indents are set and displayed, and every paragraph has its own ruler settings.

This is critical. Any tabs or indents you set in the Tabs panel will apply *only to the paragraph that is currently selected;* that is, tab settings are paragraph-specific, as explained on page 31.

Open the Tabs panel from the Type menu.

The Tabs panel displays the ruler increments that are showing in the Ruler on the page (as explained on page 10). Here you see picas (see page 20). **To see larger and more detailed increments in this ruler,** enlarge the view of the document; unfortunately, this doesn't enlarge the tiny little markers.

TASK 1   Experiment with the Tabs panel and paragraphs

1 Create a text frame three or four inches wide and type several lines of text (do not hit a Return at the ends of the lines).

2 After a couple of lines, hit a Return (which creates *a new paragraph*) and type several more lines of text.

3 While the insertion point is at the end of the *second* paragraph, go to the Type menu and choose "tabs," *or* if the tabs ruler is already on the screen, click the tiny magnet icon to snap it to the text frame.

4 Find the triangle at the far right end (that's the Right Indent marker) and drag it inward (to the left) about an inch.

The right margin in the *second* paragraph indents an inch inward because *that is the paragraph that is selected.*

Notice that the first paragraph did *not* indent its right margin.

5 Now single-click in the *first* paragraph to set the insertion point within that paragraph.

In the Tabs panel, you see that the Right Indent marker (the triangle) is back in its original position. That's because every paragraph has its own settings.

To change the settings of more than one paragraph at once, select all the paragraphs you want to change. (These paragraphs must be *contiguous,* or connected to each other, to select them.)

B **The Tabs panel ruler has invisible tab settings every half inch.**

I put colored dots on the image to represent the invisible default tab markers.

As soon as you set your own tab, every default tab setting to the left of that new tab disappears.

However, any tabs that you manually set will not disappear.

TASK 2   Experiment with a tab marker

1   Make sure the Ruler across the top of the screen is showing (from the View menu).

Make sure the Ruler is in inches for now. If it isn't displaying inches, you can change it: Control-click or right-click on the Ruler; from the menu that appears, choose "Inches."

2   Create a text frame three or four inches wide.

3   Hit the Tab key, then type a silly word, such as *Dogfood*.

4   If the Tabs panel is open, single-click on its magnet icon to make it snap to the text frame you just made. *Or* open the Tabs panel (from the Type menu), and it will position itself directly over the text box. The word you typed is aligned with the half-inch mark.

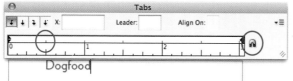

Click the magnet icon to snap the Tabs panel to the selected text frame.

5   Single-click in the Tabs panel ruler near the 2-inch mark; the word you typed will instantly jump to that new marker because all the invisible default tab settings to its left have disappeared.

Drag that tab marker left or right and watch the word snap to that new position.

C Tabs are cumulative, and they accumulate in the word you type after you hit the Tab key.

Huh? Well, if you hit the Tab key three times and then type the word *Rosalind,* that word *Rosalind* holds onto those three tabs. *Rosalind* will jump over to the third tab *she can find* (which does not necessarily mean the third tab in the Tabs panel!).

If you then hit two more tabs and type the word *Celia,* the word *Celia* holds onto *five* tabs—the tabs accumulate. And again, *Celia* will jump to the fifth tab *she can find.*

I say "the fifth tab she can find" because perhaps *Rosalind's* name is too long and extends past the fourth tab in the ruler; in that case, *Celia* doesn't count that tab—she only counts two more beyond *Rosalind,* the two she can find.

This is probably the most crazy-making thing about tabs, so spend a couple of minutes to understand it and control it.

TASK 3 Experiment with accumulating tabs

1 Create a text frame four to six inches wide.

2 Follow these directions precisely (that is, do *not* type more than one tab between words).

Hit the Tab key once.
Type *Cat,* then hit the Tab key once.
Type *Dog,* then hit the Tab key once.
Type *Rhinoceros,* then hit the Tab key once.
Type *Ape,* then hit the Tab key once.

Hit the Enter key to create a new paragraph.

Hit the Tab key once.
Type *Rat,* then hit the Tab key once.
Type *Bird,* then hit the Tab key once.
Type *Shrew,* then hit the Tab key once.
Type *Monkey* (even if it doesn't line up!), then hit the Tab key once.

3 **To see the tab markers,** go to the Type menu and choose "Show Hidden Characters." You will see one tab marker before each word.

You can see there is one tab marker (») pushing each word to the right, to align with the default tabs set every half inch.

Here's the critical thing to notice in the example:

Cat went to the first tab it could find, at ½ inch.

Dog went to the second tab it could find, at 1 inch.

Rhinoceros went to the third tab it could find, at 1.5 inches.

Ape went to the fourth tab *it could find.* Now, the fourth (default and invisible) tab in the Tabs panel ruler is at 2 inches, but *Ape* couldn't get to that one because *Rhinoceros* is in the way. Thus it had to go to the next one it could find.

In the second paragraph, all four words are able to line up at the half-inch default tab markers.

To make all four columns align so you can carry on with your lists, all you need to do is *create new tab markers that replace the defaults,* giving the words room enough. Follow the steps below.

4 Select both paragraphs: With the Text tool, press-and-drag to select the text in both lines, or press Command A (PC: Control A). You don't have to select *every* word in both lines, just a few letters in each.

5 Make sure the **left-aligned tab marker** is selected, as circled below.

Single-click in the Tabs panel ruler where you want the tab to be. For instance, put the first tab at ½ inch. Nothing will change.

Put the second tab at about 1.25 inches. The words that have accumulated two tabs, *Dog* and *Bird,* will move to that new second tab.

Put the third tab at about 2 inches. Put the fourth tab at about 3 inches. All of the words will instantly align with the tab they are looking for. They will go exactly where you tell them.

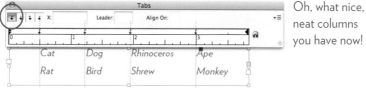

Oh, what nice, neat columns you have now!

Notice that **as you manually set a tab marker, the default and invisible markers every half-inch *to the left* disappear** (they remain every half-inch to the *right* of the last manual tab marker). You can tell they are no longer in place because tabbed text doesn't stop there.

Continue to experiment: Select both paragraphs, and drag the tab markers left and right; watch everything follow along. Hit Enter and type another line of four animals; adjust the tabs if necessary.

D **You can remove extra tabs in the text just as if the tabs were characters.**

One reason why tabs can be so confusing is that not only are the default tab markers in the ruler invisible, but the characters in the text are invisible. As you saw in Step 3, you can "Show Hidden Characters" to see them.

Here you can clearly see the three tab characters that *James* is obeying, and you can see that *Ryan* has accumulated five tabs.

Even when you cannot see the actual tab characters, you can remove them just as if they were letters. If you had typed three periods in front of the words "James Clifton," you know how to delete those periods. In exactly the same way, you can delete tab characters.

TASK 4   Delete tabs from the text

1   Create a text frame about four or five inches wide.

2   Hit the Tab key three times, then type *James Clifton.*
    Hit the Tab key two more times, then type *Ryan Nigel.*

3   Click to set the insertion point in front of *James Clifton.*
    Drag a wee bit to the left, just enough to select the chunk of tab.
    You will notice that you cannot select only a portion of that tab
    character—it's all or nothing.

4   Hit the Delete key. Watch how *James Clifton* now goes to the second
    tab he can find. When you delete one tab from *James,* notice that *Ryan*
    also has one less tab; he now goes to the fourth tab he can find.

Tab alignments and symbols

InDesign provides four tab alignments, and each one has its own symbol.

When you hit the Tab key and it goes to a **left-aligned tab,** the insertion point goes to the tab marker and the text types to the right (it aligns on the left). Notice the visual clue of the direction of the tail on the symbol—it shows you which direction the type will head.

When you hit the Tab key and it goes to a **right-aligned tab,** the insertion point goes to the tab marker and the text types to the left (it aligns on the right).

When you hit the Tab key and it goes to a **centered tab,** the insertion point goes to the tab marker and the text types outward on both sides of the marker.

When you hit the Tab key and it goes to a **decimal tab,** the insertion point goes to the tab marker. The text extends to the left *until* you type a decimal (a period), then the text continues on the other side, typing to the right.

The following pages walk you through exercises to become familiar with these tabs. As I've mentioned before, it is worth your time to become proficient!

> **TIP:** Before you do the exercises, make sure your Tabs panel has no prior defaults set. Use the panel menu to "Clear All" and "Restore Indents" if necessary.

Tab basics

- **The ruler across the top of the document window has nothing to do with tabs.** Do not try to align your text by measuring in that ruler! The only way the ruler across the top of the document and the Tabs panel ruler are related is that the horizontal measurement you choose in the document ruler changes the measurement in the Tabs panel ruler.

- The Tabs panel ruler applies to the **selected** text frame or the **selected** text.

- Every **paragraph** has its own tab settings.

- Always use a **left alignment** with tabs! If you set tabs and it's all messed up, check to make sure the text alignment is left-aligned.

- You can **set up tabs** before you begin typing, or type some text and then add the tabs.

- **To add a tab marker** to the Tabs panel ruler, single-click the type of tab you want (explained on the previous page), then single-click in the Tabs panel ruler to set the tab marker.

- **To move a tab marker,** drag the marker left or right.

- **To delete a tab marker,** drag the marker off the ruler— up, down, or diagonally.

- **To change the tab marker to another alignment,** single-click on the marker you want to change. Then single-click on the symbol for the type of tab you want to replace it with.

- If you open the Tabs panel and set tab markers when there is no text selected and no frame selected, the tabs you set will be the **new defaults.** That is, any new text frame you create in that document will have those tab settings. Take advantage of this!

- **To clear all tab markers** and return the invisible defaults at every half inch, use the panel menu and choose "Clear tabs."

TIP: When working with tabs, get in the habit of NEVER hitting more than one tab to get to the column you want. Trust me, typing extra tabs is only crazy-making when you want to format the text.

A Mid summer Night's Dream

at the Scottish Rite Temple
Santa Fe • June 24 2011

presented by

SANTA FE *Shakespeare* **SOCIETY**

SANTA FE *Shakespeare* SOCIETY

The Santa Fe Shakespeare Society is a nonprofit organization dedicated to increasing the enjoyment, understanding, and appreciation of Shakespeare's works through readings, performance, commentary, and educational activities.

A Midsummer Night's Dream

Director: Jerry Ferraccio
Narrator: Michael Graves

The Warriors

Hippolyta, Queen of the Amazons, engaged to Theseus .... Laura Egley Taylor
Theseus, Duke of Athens, engaged to Hippolyta .... Andrew Tree

The Courtiers

Egeus, father of Hermia .... Chuck Maynard
Philostrate, Master of Revels to the Athenian Court .... Sherry Engstrom

The Lovers

Hermia, in love with Lysander .... Rosalía Tríana
Lysander, in love with Hermia .... Patrick Briggs
Helena, in love with Demetrius .... Ramsey Scott
Demetrius, initially in love with Hermia, and Egeus' choice for her husband .... Jerry Ferraccio

The Mechanicals

Athenian laborers who intend to present a play for Theseus and Hippolyta's wedding festivities

Peter Quince, a carpenter and organizer of the play; he speaks the Prologue ...... Stefany Burrowes
Nick Bottom, a weaver who plays Pyramus .... Meg Hachmann
Francis Flute, a bellows-mender who plays Thisbe .... Hedy Parks
Tom Snout, a tinker who plays Wall .... Sherry Engstrom
Snug, a joiner who plays the Lion .... Charles Maynard
Robin Starveling, a tailor who plays the Moon .... Kelly Kiernan

The Supernaturals

Puck (also called Robin Goodfellow), Oberon's attendant and jester .... Ron Weisberg
Oberon, King of the Fairies .... Kelly Kiernan
Titania, Queen of the Fairies .... Laura Egley Taylor
Titania's attendants:
    Peaseblossom .... Hedy Beinert
    Cobweb .... Andrew Tree
    Moth .... Charles Maynard
    Mustardseed .... Sherry Engstrom

Knowing how to use your tabs and indents makes it very easy to create something like a theater program. Spacing control also helps immensely.

Left-aligned tabs

A left-aligned tab is the most commonly used, where the text aligns on the left side and moves out to the right, just as you expect when you type or write in English. If you did Task 3 on page 66, you were using left-aligned tabs. Here is another small exercise.

TASK 5 Create a chart using left-aligned tabs

1 Create a new text frame about five or six inches wide.

2 Type the text below. Do NOT hit a tab at the beginning of each line; only hit the Tab key before the words *True* and *False*. As shown below, the text will not align, but that's okay, as long as *True* has one tab and *False* has another tab.

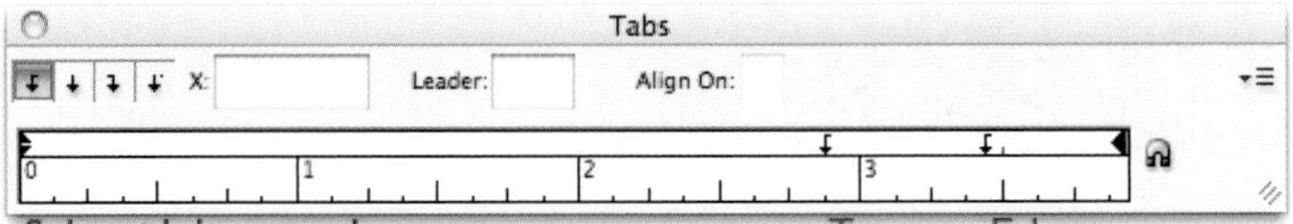

Solpugids have ten legs. True False
Solpugids are related to Harvestmen. True False
Solpugids belong to the order of Solifugids. True False
Solpugids cannot kill you. True False
Solpugids liquefy their prey. True False

3 Select all the text.

4 Open the Tabs panel if it isn't already. If necessary, click the magnet icon to snap the panel to the text frame.

5 Click the left-aligned tab marker.

6 Single-click in the ruler at a position beyond the end of the longest question. That new tab marker deletes all the default tabs to its left, so now all the *Trues* jump to that first tab marker.

All the *Falses* jump to the *second* tab marker, which will be the next default they can find. Click in the ruler to set another tab a little farther to the right. Feel free to move them around!

Solpugids have ten legs. » True » False¶
Solpugids are related to Harvestmen. » True » False¶
Solpugids belong to the order of Solifugids. » True » False¶
Solpugids cannot kill you. » True » False¶
Solpugids liquefy their prey. » True » False#

TASK 6 Create another chart using left-aligned tabs

This exercise is different from the previous one only in that you are going to set the tabs *before* you begin typing.

1 Create a text frame about five inches wide.

2 With the insertion point flashing in the text frame (which means that text frame is selected), open the Tabs panel (from the Type menu, *or* use the keyboard shortcut (Command Shift T or PC: Control Shift T).

3 Set tabs at .75 inch and 2.5 inch.

4 Choose a font size of 10 point.

5 Type the text shown below.

After the first paragraph of body copy *("Below is a list . . . "),* hit tabs before the headings and the entries in the "Relation" and "RSVP yes" columns.

Hit Enter at the end of each row.

At any point, select all of the text and move the tab markers as necessary.

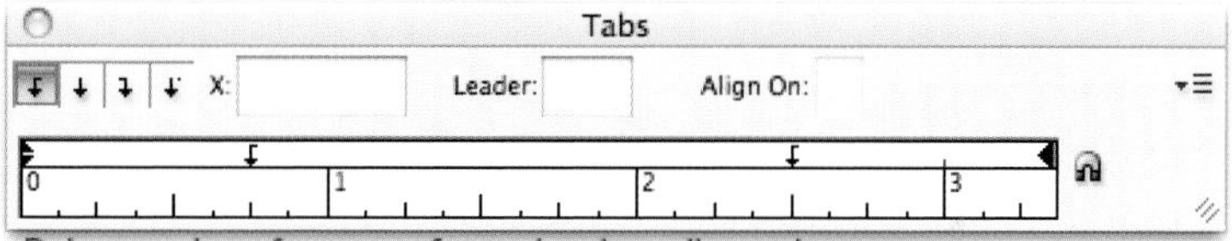

Below is a list of names of people who will join the party in Messina on July 6:

Name	Relation	RSVP yes
Antonio	Governor	•
Hero	Daughter of Governor	•
Beatrice	Niece of Governor	•
Don Pedro	Prince of Aragon	•
Don John	Bastard brother of Don Pedro	
Claudio	Aristrocratic soldier	•
Benedick	Aristrocratic soldier	•

If the hidden characters are showing, you should see one tab symbol before the "Relation" column and another tab symbol before the "RSVP yes" column.

TIP: If you want to center "RSVP yes" over the column of bullets, single-click with the Text tool in that line of type. Drag the tab marker to the left until the text is centered over that column.

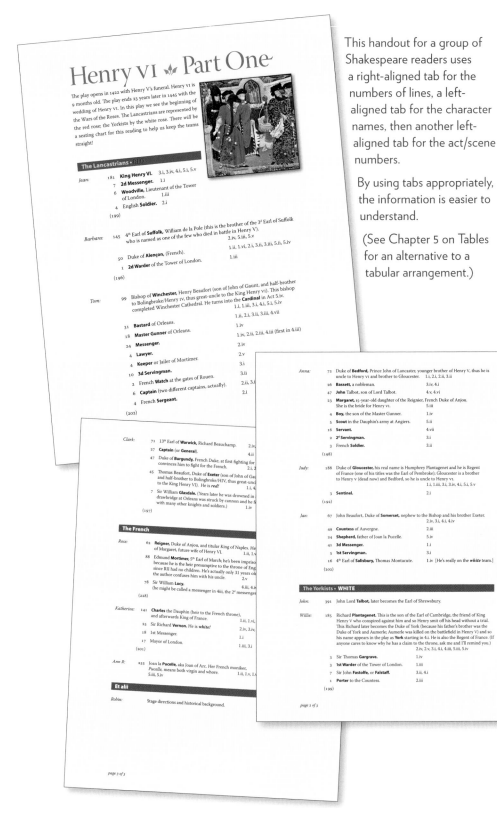

This handout for a group of Shakespeare readers uses a right-aligned tab for the numbers of lines, a left-aligned tab for the character names, then another left-aligned tab for the act/scene numbers.

By using tabs appropriately, the information is easier to understand.

(See Chapter 5 on Tables for an alternative to a tabular arrangement.)

Right-aligned tabs

Right-aligned tabs are useful for numbers that don't have a decimal point, or for any items that you want to align on the right.

TASK 7 Create a numbered chart using right-aligned tabs

This exercise involves whole numbers. You'll type a few lines with tabs before you set up the markers.

1 Create a new text frame about five inches wide.

2 Type the following text in 10-point type, hitting the Tab key *once* to move to the next column, whether it aligns or not at this point. Hit Enter or Return at the end of each line.

Thomas Middleton, The Witch

Act:	I	II	III	IV	V	Total
Hecate	158	—	52	—	58	268

3 Select all the text.

4 Open the Tabs panel. *Or* if it is already open, single-click the magnet icon so the panel snaps to the text frame.

5 If there are any tab markers in the ruler, click the tiny menu symbol at the right end of the panel (circled, below) and choose "Clear All" (this clears any tabs you added and restores the invisible defaults).

Single-click the right-aligned tab symbol (circled below, left).

6 Single-click six tab markers, starting at about 1 inch. Watch the text numbers align appropriately.

7 Continue typing to finish the chart, as shown below.

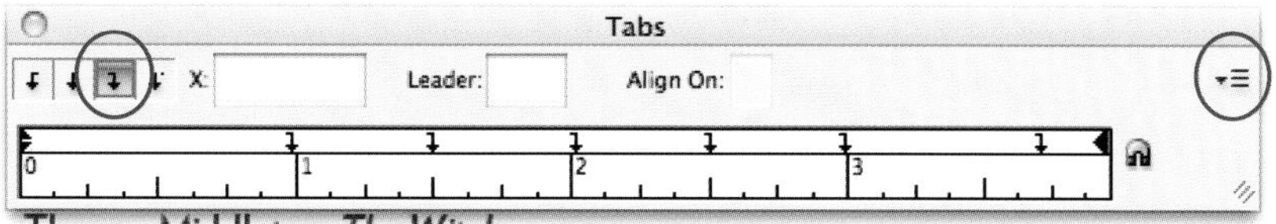

Thomas Middleton, *The Witch*

Act:	I	II	III	IV	V	Total
Hecate	158	—	52	—	58	268
Sebastian	47	23	64	89	22	245
Francisca	4	100	56	62	—	222
Isabella	1	50	80	27	20	178
Aberzane	—	71	8	—	17	96

Decimal-aligned tabs

The decimal tab does not just align decimal points in numbers—you can assign any character to align. For instance, you might want the dollar signs to align, or the right brackets, or a bullet.

TASK 8 Align text to a decimal point

This exercise involves numbers with the decimal point in various places.

1 Create a new text frame about five inches wide.

2 Type the following text in 10-point type, hitting the Tab key *once* to move to the next column, whether it aligns or not at this point. Hit Enter or Return at the end of each line.

PERCENTAGE OF ALIENS LIVING ON PLANET EARTH

Original Planet	% of U.S. Population	Years on Earth
Tralfamadore	7.03	1378.23
Kobol	4.006	412.2
Gallifrey	1.52	901.6
Naboo	.76	1277.71
Oerth	.413	87.3

3 Select the heading line ("Original Planet," etc.) and set left-aligned tabs for the two headings that label the numbers columns.

4 Select the lines with numbers and set decimal tabs so the numbers are visually centered under their headings (choose the decimal tab symbol, then click in the ruler).

Rather than set a tab in front of each line, I indented these lines by dragging both of the left markers in the ruler to the right a wee bit, as you can see above (see pages 82–86 about the indent markers).

TASK 9   Align text to a character

Don't limit yourself to aligning text on a period. When you use a decimal tab, it actually aligns the text according to the symbol that is in the "Align On" field, which by default is a period. But you can type or paste any character into that little field and have your text align with it.

1   Create a text frame about 3 inches wide; choose 10-point type.

2   Type the text below, hitting a tab at the *beginning* of each line. At the moment, the tab will go to the default ½-inch marker. That's okay.

   To type the heart in Zapf Dingbats, see pages 36–37 on using the Glyphs panel (or feel free to use any dingbat you want).

3   Open the Tabs panel and click the magnet to snap it to the frame.

4   Select all the text.

5   Single-click on the decimal tab to select it. Once it is selected, the "Align On" field is available.

   Copy the heart from the text; click in the "Align On" field and paste it in. All the heart symbols are aligned. (If they are not aligned, show the hidden characters to make sure you hit a tab at the beginning of each line.)

TIP: Once tabs are set in a line of text, you can hit the Enter key to type the next line and the tabs will continue to carry on in the same format.

Right-aligned tabs with leaders

"Leaders" are the dots or lines that lead your eye from one column to another, most often seen in tables of contents. When working with leaders, remember that the tab marker holds on to the leader specs, so if you delete that tab, you delete the leaders.

TASK 10   Create tabs with leaders

1   Create a text frame about 3 inches wide; choose 10-point type.

2   Type the first line or two of the list shown below, hitting a tab before the page number. Do *not* type the dots!

3   Select the text.

4   Open the Tabs panel and click the magnet to snap it to the frame.

5   Single-click the right-aligned tab; click in the Tabs panel ruler close to the right edge.

6   While that tab is still selected, type the leader character that you want to use in the "Leader" field. For now, type a period. You will instantly see the leaders connect from the name to the number, which is now right-aligned as well.

7   Click at the end of the last line (after the number) to put your insertion point in that position. Hit Enter to make a new paragraph.

Continue typing the rest of the list. As long as you keep hitting the Enter (or Return) key at the end of each line (which turns that line into a paragraph), the tab formatting will carry over to the next line.

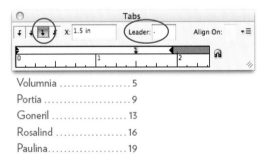

TIP: You can type or paste any character into the "Leader" field. In fact, you can use up to eight characters. Experiment with this!

TASK 11 Match the leaders

One sign of unprofessional typography is when the leaders in a list have differently sized dots. This happens because the leader automatically picks up the formatting from the last character before the tab, as shown below-left. You can see the consistent formatting for leaders and page numbers in the example, below-right.

Ceramic Tiles **5**		**Ceramic Tiles** 5		
Handmade ceramic 6		Handmade ceramic 6		
Unglazed porcelain. 9		Unglazed porcelain. 9		
Recycled broken pottery . . . 13		Recycled broken pottery . . . 13		
Glass tiles **15**		**Glass tiles** 15		
Recycled glass 18		Recycled glass 18		
Smalti 23		Smalti 23		
Millefiori 26		Millefiori 26		

1 Recreate the text above, using a heavy bold face for the headings. Set the right-aligned tab with leaders, as explained on the opposite page.

2 The leaders are simply formatted characters, so there are several ways to make the leaders match. Experiment with these options:

- Select the leaders in each line and change the formatting (to 8-point Light, for instance).

- *Or* select the smaller leaders in one of the lines.
  Copy the leaders.
  Select the larger leaders in one of the headings.
  Paste. Paste to replace the others as well.

- *Or* create a style sheet for character formatting, as explained in Chapter 6. Assign a keyboard shortcut to it, then apply it to the selected leaders.

- *Or* create a paragraph style sheet with nested character styles, as explained in Chapter 6, so the leaders and the page numbers appear in the proper formatting automatically.

- *Or* if you use the Table of Contents feature (from the Layout menu), your paragraph and character style sheets will be applied automatically as InDesign generates your table of contents. You can see an example in this book's contents—the entire table was formatted when I clicked the button. Unfortunately, I don't have room in this small book to explain InDesign's book features, but they are in the Adobe online manual.

Right- and left-align the text

Have you ever wanted to put a header across the top of a page where the text aligns both on the left and the right sides? Here's the trick:

TASK 12 Create a header aligned on both sides

1 Create a one-line text frame that stretches across the column.

2 Type the text you want to align on the left.

3 Hit a tab.

4 Type the text you want to align on the right.

5 Select the line (your insertion point in the line selects it).

6 Right-justify the line: In the Paragraph panel, single-click the *Align right* icon.

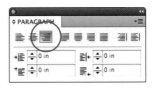

PROPOSAL · JAN NELSON   PAGE 3

Now you can widen or narrow the frame and the text will always align. If you want this text on every page in your document, put the frame on the master page, as explained on pages 14–15.

The Repeat tab

I love this feature. You can create a series of tabs across the frame that are exactly the same distance apart from each other. Try this small task:

TASK 13 Repeat a typographic element

1 Type a bullet or an ornament over and over, hitting a tab between each one.

2 Set a tab in the Tabs panel ruler, and make sure it is selected.

3 From the panel menu on the right end of the ruler, choose "Repeat tab." *The distance between each tab will be the distance from the selected tab and the tab or margin to its left.*

4 To change the spacing, select the tab, move it left or right, then choose "Repeat tab" again.

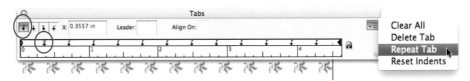

Try this!

Here is a small exercise that utilizes both left- and right-aligned tabs in a practical situation. Format the text in A so it looks like the text in B.

A Memo

To: Mistress Quickly

From: Ann Page

Subject: Marry him?

Date: May 1, 1594

Alas, my mother insists that I marry that old crank, Doctor Caius! Mistress Quickly, help me—I had rather be set quick in the earth and bowled to death with turnips!

B

MEMO

        To: Mistress Quickly
      From: Ann Page
    Subject: Marry him?
      Date: May 1, 1594

Alas, my mother insists that I marry that old crank, Doctor Caius! Mistress Quickly, help me—I had rather be set quick in the earth and bowled to death with turnips!

In this short piece, I also adjusted the spacing between the lines and paragraphs (as explained in Chapter 3) to help clarify the communication.

Indent the text

Indents are easier to understand than tabs, as long as you know that each paragraph has its own Tabs panel ruler settings.

There are three indent markers:

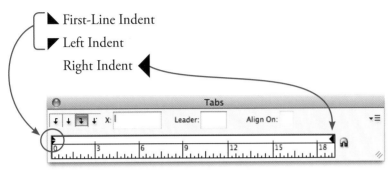

The Tabs panel ruler, as you know by now, snaps to the *selected* text frame (selected with either the black Selection tool or by clicking the Type tool inside the text frame). The text frame itself creates the **margins.** The left and right **indents** *indent the text in relation to those margins, or edges, of the text frame.* The indents have nothing to do with the ruler across the top of the window nor with the document margins!

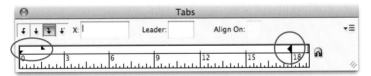

Here you can see that the First-Line Indent marker has been moved to the right, and the Right Indent has been moved to the left.

The indents make perfect sense if you just remember this:

The text in a paragraph begins at the **First-Line Indent** marker.

As you type, the text moves to the right and at the end of the line bumps into the **Right Indent** marker (as long as you don't hit a Return or the Enter key).

After it hits the Right Indent, the text bounces back to the **Left Indent** marker (the bottom triangle) and carries on, bouncing back and forth between the Right and Left Indent markers.

As soon as you hit Enter or Return, the line starts over again at the **First-Line Indent** marker.

TASK 14 Experiment with the indents

This exercise involves playing with the indents. As you move the markers, watch the text move. Get to a point where you can predict what will happen as you move the markers.

1 Create a small text frame, about 3 x 3 inches.

2 Choose a font, choose 10-point type, and justify the text.

3 From the Type menu, choose "Fill with Placeholder Text" (it's toward the bottom of the menu). Divide the text into three paragraphs (click to set the insertion point, then hit Enter).

> Fuga, bearianditis quatem at omni hicae. Bore pre ndi cipsunt, que natem fuga. Ut occulla prorias core plit volup taquo teni re.
>
> Voluptatur sum desti ilit ut res as doluptia voluptam, offic tet maior ehenis earum velectibus aute nim am, sus aut precto te vellis.
>
> Olorpos explate sam elenditatium estotate eos volenihitias ut es aut harchicid magni corrovid quidende volorendam ex exero offic tesed unt eture, offic to volorem sam eum est, volor sit.

Your text will look something like this.

To get a little extra space between the paragraphs, use the "Paragraph Space After" field (see page 55).

4 Select all the text, then open the Tabs panel; if it's already open, click the magnet icon to snap the ruler to the text frame.

5 **Drag the First-Line Indent marker** (the top triangle on the left) inward toward the right. Only the first lines will indent.

6 **Drag the Right Indent marker** in toward the left; the right side of the text will indent itself *from the edge of the text frame.*

Experiment with the margin: Choose the black Selection tool; single-click on the text frame. Drag the right edge of the text frame to the right, then to the left. Notice that the Right Indent is always the same proportional distance from the right edge of the text frame.

7 Get the Type tool again, and **drag the Left Indent marker** in toward the right. Notice it automatically drags the First-Line Indent marker with it! This is so the indent and margin remain in proportion.

To drag the Left Indent marker by itself, hold down the Shift key and drag the marker.

8 Now select individual paragraphs and change the indents.

9 When you can move a marker and predict what will happen, reset the indents: Select all the text, then from the Tabs panel menu, choose "Reset Indents."

TASK 15 Create a hanging indent

This is a setting you'll use all the time, where you have something like a bullet or a name that begins the line, but you want the text to align with the main body copy, not under the bullet. It's easier than you might think.

1 In a text frame, type something like the lines below. After the bullet, hit a tab to start the text.

> •   **Lindy Hop** developed in the late 1920s from the Charleston. It has an 8-count basic and an emphasis on improvisation. You can dance the Lindy Hop to almost every style of music.
> •   **Balboa** emphasizes quick footwork and a close embrace for crowded floors. It is usually danced to fast jazz, though you can Balboa to slower tempos.
> •   **Jitterbug** is actually a term coined by Cab Calloway that describes the dancer, not the dance; that is, a jitterbug might dance the Lindy Hop, Charleston, Shag, or any other swing dance.

2 Select all the text, then open the Tabs panel; if it's already open, click the magnet icon to snap the panel to the frame.

3 You can see, above, that the first line, beginning with the bullet, starts where the Left Indent marker is set, all the way to the left. The text begins at the first tab stop, probably the default half-inch mark. What we want is for the text, after it bounces off the right edge, to align with the first words. All it takes is one small move.

Hold down the Shift key and drag the **Left Indent** marker, the lower triangle on the left, to about the ¼-inch mark on the ruler. (If a tab marker appears, drag it off the ruler and try again.) The Left Indent marker acts as the first tab, so everything lines up at once.

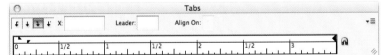

• **Lindy Hop** developed in the late 1920s from the Charleston. It has an 8-count basic and an emphasis on improvisation. You can dance the Lindy Hop to almost every style of music.
• **Balboa** emphasizes quick footwork and a close embrace for crowded floors. It is usually danced to fast jazz, though you can Balboa to slower tempos.
• **Jitterbug** is actually a term coined by Cab Calloway that describes the *dancer*, not the dance; that is, a jitterbug might dance the Lindy Hop, Charleston, Shag, or any other swing dance.

In this example, I also moved the First-Line Indent a wee bit so the bullet is closer to the text.

TASK 16 Create a numbered indent

You can see that the setting on the opposite page will work for a numbered list, right? Type the number, hit the tab, type the text; after you hit Enter, start over again.

But when the list goes above 9 items, the numbers are no longer aligned properly. This is a sure sign of unprofessional type. The trick is that you must type a tab *before* the number so it aligns on the right, then type a tab *after* the number to get to the text.

1   In a text frame, type the first line of the list below. Make sure to hit the Tab key *before* you type the number, as well as *after* the number.

2   Select all the text, and open the Tabs panel.

3   Click the right-aligned or decimal tab symbol, then click in the ruler at about the ¼-inch mark.

4   Hold down the Shift key and drag the Left Indent marker a little way past the tab, to its right.

5   Hit a Return or Enter at the end of the first line of text, and carry on with typing the rest of the list. Don't forget those two tabs!

6   At any point, select all the text and adjust the tab and indent markers as necessary.

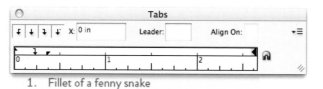

1.   Fillet of a fenny snake
2.   Eye of newt and toe of frog
3.   Wool of bat and tongue of dog
4.   Adder's fork and blindworm's sting
5.   Lizard's leg and howlet's wing
6.   Scale of dragon
7.   Tooth of wolf
8.   Witches' mummy
9.   Maw and gulf of the ravined salt-sea shark
10.   Root of hemlock digged in the dark
11.   Nose of Turk
12.   Tartar's lips
13.   Finger of birth-strangled babe, ditch-delivered by a drab

You can see that when you hit Enter, the text goes all the way back to the left, to the First-Line Indent marker.

You hit the Tab key and the insertion point aligns at the tab marker. Type the number.

You hit the Tab key and the insertion point jumps to the Left Indent marker, which doubles as a tab.

When you hit Return, it starts over again.

Automatic bullets and numbering

InDesign has a **Bullets and Numbering** feature that will number a list for you automatically. This is enormously helpful because you can rearrange the list, add new items, delete items, and the entire list is automatically renumbered.

This feature does not align the numbers appropriately, as shown below-left, but this might be a small price to pay when you have a long list.

TASK 17 Use automatic numbering

1 Create a text frame and type the first word or two in a list.

2 With the insertion point flashing in that first line, go to the Type menu and choose "Bulleted & Numbered Lists…," then choose "Apply Numbers."

3 The number 1 will appear at the beginning of the line. Hit Return or Enter and continue on with your list.

4 To remove the numbers or switch to a bulleted list, go back to the menu and choose the option you want.

5 For more control over the formatting, select all the text in the list. From the Paragraph panel menu, choose "Bullets and Numbering," then experiment with the options.

Also use the formatting options you learned in this chapter!

1. Ablutophobia: Fear of washing or bathing.
2. Chorophobia: Fear of dancing.
3. Didaskaleinophobia: Fear of going to school.
4. Ergophobia: Fear of work.
5. Geniophobia: Fear of chins.
6. Hippopotomonstrosesquipedaliophobia: Fear of long words.
7. Lachanophobia: Fear of vegetables.
8. Macrophobia: Fear of long waits.
9. Myxophobia: Fear of slime.
10. Pluviophobia: Fear of rain or of being rained on.
11. Soceraphobia: Fear of in-laws.
12. Xanthophobia: Fear of the color yellow or the word yellow.
13. Zemmiphobia: Fear of the Great Mole Rat.

The numbers are aligned properly, ones in the ones place and tens in the tens place. The text is also aligned properly.

1. Ablutophobia: Fear of washing or bathing.
2. Chorophobia: Fear of dancing.
3. Didaskaleinophobia: Fear of going to school.
4. Ergophobia: Fear of work.
5. Geniophobia: Fear of chins.
6. Hippopotomonstrosesquipedaliophobia: Fear of long words.
7. Lachanophobia: Fear of vegetables.
8. Macrophobia: Fear of long waits.
9. Myxophobia: Fear of slime.
10. Pluviophobia: Fear of rain or of being rained on.
11. Soceraphobia: Fear of in-laws.
12. Xanthophobia: Fear of the color yellow or the word yellow.
13. Zemmiphobia: Fear of the Great Mole Rat.

You can fix the issue shown in lines 6, 10, and 12: Use the Tabs panel (move the Left Indent to align with the tab marker).

Try this!

On this page and the next are examples of things you can do if you know how to control your tabs and indents. Use these as exercises to experiment with what you know!

Meet the Staff

Paulina's insightful human awareness and communication skills will help steer you toward more fulfilling career options. Discover possibilities for yourself that you didn't know existed!

Beatrice has a remarkable capacity for the written and spoken word. She will help craft your résumés and presentations to best showcase your skills.

Rosalind's knowledge of today's market makes her a most effective guide. She will lead you through the job-search process to find a perfect position for yourself.

This is exactly the same format as the hanging indent on page 84, except instead of a bullet, I placed a graphic at that insertion point (see page 219 for a brief intro to anchored objects).

As I edit the text, the photos flow along in position.

Also experiment with using beautiful ornaments instead of bullets.

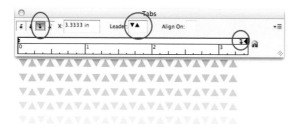

There are so many ways to use tabs. In this example, I put a right-aligned tab close to the right edge, and used two Zapf Dingbats characters as leaders, as shown above (I copied and pasted them in). Then I simply hit the Tab key, Enter, tab, Enter, tab, Enter, etc. I colored the leaders as you would color any text.

Here are a couple more common uses of the tabs and indents. You already learned the basics of how to create these earlier in this chapter.

Name _____

Address_____

City_____

State/Zip _____

Phone _____

Name..

Address......................................

City...

State/Zip....................................

Phone..

These lines are simply right-aligned tabs with leaders, which creates a perfectly aligned edge on the right.

Instead of creating lines using *Shift _* across the page, set a right-aligned tab at the end of the line and type *Shift _* into the "Leaders" field. *Or* use a period and a space as the leader, and then reduce the point size (as explained on page 79).

Fruit	Price	Quantity	Total
Bananas	.83	12	$9.96
Apples	.49	6	$2.94
Kiwis	.98	22	$22.56

If you're feeling confident, add a new column between two existing columns, as shown below.

Fruit	Price	Qty	Date	Total
Bananas	.83	12	8/17	$9.96
Apples	.49	6	9/23	$2.94
Kiwis	.98	22	11/6	$22.56

This little piece uses right-aligned and decimal tabs. Remember, each paragraph can have its own ruler settings, so the first line here (which is considered a paragraph) has different tabs: the first and last are right-aligned, the others are visually centered over the columns.

As long as you remember that the text must have a tab in front of it so it will align with the tab marker, you can work this out. *The tabbed text will go exactly where you tell it!*

5 Tables

InDesign's tables can be gorgeous. You might think you don't need tables, but I guarantee that if you work through the tasks in this chapter, you will become enamored of tables and their possibilities. You will start thinking of work to do just so you can create a table to put it in.

One could write an entire book on the table feature in InDesign, but this chapter provides just an introduction to get you started. If you are a veteran table creator in a program like Microsoft Word, tables will make sense to you and you will perform wonders.

Any text you import from Word that includes tables will convert to InDesign text and tables just fine (you'll need to do some design tweaking). Microsoft Excel data will import into tables as well.

There are no individual **tasks** in this chapter because everything builds on what went before. So I suggest you start at the beginning and carry on to the end, and then you will know how to build tables!

When to use a table

Tables are fabulous for when you need to create columns of data, but tabs are too limited. You can create an entire project in tables, as shown on the opposite page, or you might want to embed a small table into an existing document. An embedded table will move with the rest of the text as you edit it.

In a table, text is typed into individual *cells,* and these cells expand as you type. Within a cell you can put any amount of text, graphics, or even other tables. You can choose to have a wide variety of borders around individual cells, groups of cells, the entire table—or no borders at all.

A table must be inserted within a text frame; you cannot create a table without first creating a text frame.

Each one of these little containers (a total of 16 in this example) is a **cell** *within the* **table***.*

Each cell can have its own border, text, graphics, and background color.

This is the text frame in which the table is built.

You can see there are four rows in this table, and there are four columns.

The text in table cells is not threaded from one cell to the next (as text frames in a story are threaded, as you learned in Chapter 2), so you don't have to worry when you edit text in one cell that it will affect the text in any other cell. As you add text, the cell grows deeper (not wider, but deeper).

At any point you can go back and format anything in the table, as you will see in the following tasks.

This upper section is not part of the table, but the rest of the seven-page document is one continuous table with headers.

Using tables allows you to create columns with varying depths of information.

Selecting elements of a table

As you work through the table-building process in the rest of this chapter, refer to this page when you need to select the text or cells.

All selections use the Type tool. The only time you'll use the black Selection tool is when you want to move the frame as an object or resize the text frame.

All cell selections are contiguous (touching); that is, you cannot select one cell in the bottom right plus one cell in the upper left at the same time.

Select the text in a cell	With the Type tool, select text as usual: • Press-and-drag over the characters • Double-click to select a word • Triple-click to select a paragraph • Press Command A (PC: Control A) to select all the text in the cell
Select the cell itself	With the Type tool, click in the cell, then hit the Esc key. *Or* with the Type tool, press-and-drag from inside the cell to the edge.
Select a row	With the Type tool, move the cursor to the left edge of the row; the cursor turns into a right-pointing arrow. With that right-pointing arrow, single-click on the left border and the entire row highlights in black.
Select a column	With the Type tool, move the cursor to the top edge of the column; the cursor turns into a down-pointing arrow. With the down-pointing arrow, single-click on the top edge and the entire column highlights in black.
Select more than one cell	With the Type tool, press-and-drag from one cell to another. The cells will turn black as they are selected.
Select the entire table to apply *table* formatting	With the Type tool, single-click anywhere in the table. Choose formatting from the Table Options dialog box (from the Table menu) or the Table panel.
Select the entire table to apply *text* formatting	With the Type tool, move the cursor to the upper-left corner; the cursor turns into a one-headed diagonal arrow. Single-click on the upper-left corner; the entire table, even if part of it is on another page, turns black.
Select the table to resize it	With the Type tool, move the cursor to the bottom edge, right edge, or bottom-right corner; the cursor turns into a double-headed arrow. Press-and-drag inward or outward.

Panels and menus for formatting a table

The most important thing to understand is how to select what you want to format, as explained on the opposite page. Once the item is selected properly, you can access the table formatting in four different ways, as shown below, plus you can use contextual menus with a right-click or Control-click (too many options for my pea brain, methinks). Use whichever option feels most comfortable to you, or use a combination of them.

When a cell/s in a table is selected, the **Control panel** across the top of the window displays formatting options. Hover over an item to display the **tool tip** that tells you what it does.

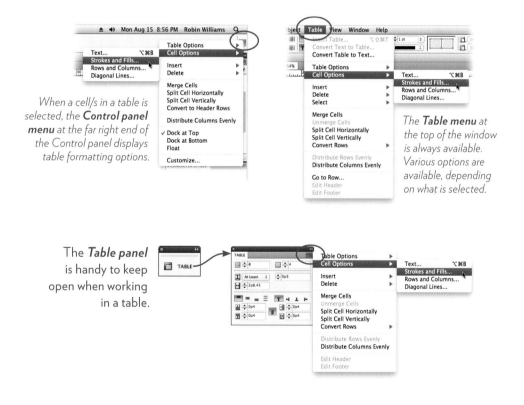

*When a cell/s in a table is selected, the **Control panel** menu at the far right end of the Control panel displays table formatting options.*

*The **Table menu** at the top of the window is always available. Various options are available, depending on what is selected.*

The **Table panel** is handy to keep open when working in a table.

TIP: You can embed a table within a table— just set your insertion point inside a cell and begin a table as usual.

Table formatting and cell formatting

You learned in Chapter 2 that there is formatting that applies to the entire paragraph (paragraph-specific) and formatting that applies only to the selected characters (character-specific). The same is true of a table—there are **table-specific options** that will apply to the entire table, and **cell-specific options** that apply only to the selected cells. Selections are made according to the chart on the previous page. Poke around in these dialog boxes for a while to familiarize yourself with the possibilities.

Settings you choose in the **Table Options** dialog box apply to the **entire table.** Click anywhere in the table to select it, then go to the Table menu and choose "Table Options," then "Table Setup…."

These options set the spacing amount above and below a table when you have embedded a table within your text, as on the previous page. This is the same as the paragraph spacing you learned about in Chapter 4.

Settings you choose in the **Cell options** apply to the **individual cells** that are selected. Select a cell or cells, then go to the Table menu and choose "Cell Options," then "Text…."

These options determine how close the text is to the borders of the cell.

To set the distances individually, click the chain-link icon to "break" the link between them all.

The following information about how to create and format tables will work most easily if you start here at the beginning and work your way through. Everything you learn in these tasks will apply to any table you create in the future.

Let's build a simple table

There are two ways to build a table: from scratch, and from existing text (select the text, then from the Table menu, choose "Convert Text to Table"). In this chapter, we're going to start from scratch.

1 With the Type tool, create a text frame about four inches across and eight inches deep.

2 From the Table menu at the top of the window, choose "Insert table…." You'll see this dialog box:

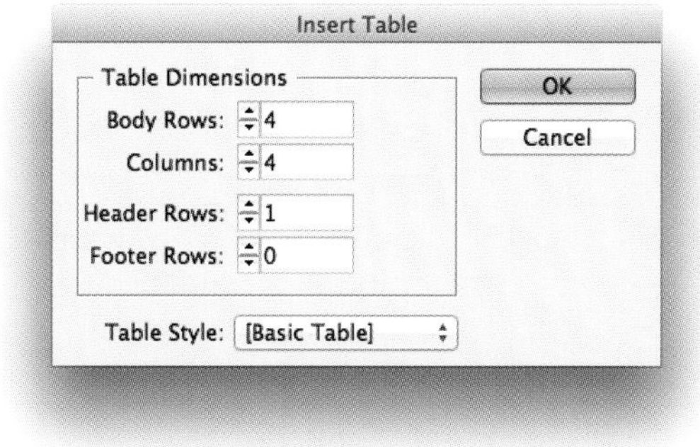

```
                    Insert Table

   ┌─ Table Dimensions ──────┐   ┌──────────┐
   │                         │   │    OK    │
   │   Body Rows:  ⇕ 4       │   └──────────┘
   │    Columns:   ⇕ 4       │   ┌──────────┐
   │                         │   │  Cancel  │
   │  Header Rows: ⇕ 1       │   └──────────┘
   │  Footer Rows: ⇕ 0       │
   └─────────────────────────┘

      Table Style:  [Basic Table]  ⇕
```

3 Enter the numbers you see above to create a table with 4 rows, 4 columns, and 1 header row.

A **header row** is a special row that always appears at the top of the table. If your table spans several pages, this exact header will duplicate itself on each page.

Click OK. A table appears on your screen with these specifications (as shown below), and it is the width of the text frame you created.

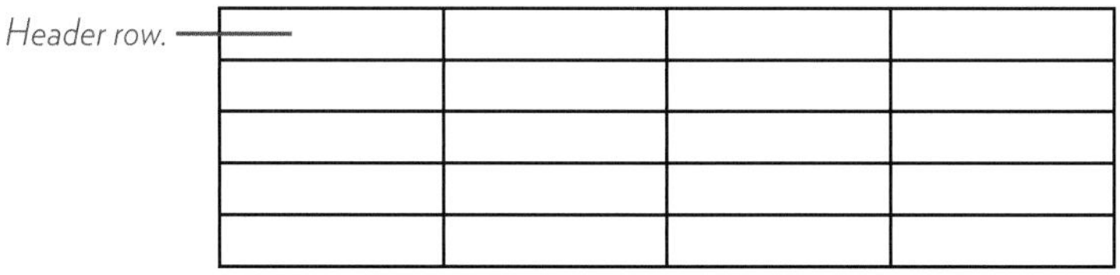

Header row. ───

> **TIP:** If you have either the black or white Selection tool chosen, double-click in the text in any cell and it will **switch to the Type tool.**

4　Enter the following information into your table, as shown below. You can, of course, enter any other data you prefer: sports teams, music groups, your relatives, favorite books, etc., with your own headings in the header row. Don't worry about the text formatting for now, except to make sure your font is small enough to fit into the cells (10-point should be great).

If you run out of space, get the black Selection tool, click on the Table to show its text frame, and drag the bottom handle on the text frame as low as necessary.

To move the table, drag it with the black Selection tool.

If you end up with a **red dot in a cell** and all your text disappears, just press on that column edge and drag it to the right.

Planet	Region	Inhabitants	Terrain
Tralfamadore	Black Garterbelt	Plumber's friends topped by a hand with a green eye in the palm	Very rocky, with water
K-PAX	D-OXON	Worm-beings, Amps, Rulis, and humanoid Dremers	Cultivated land with many medicinal herbs
Oerth	Greyspace	Dragons and Heroes	Continents, oceans, and islands
Naboo	Mid-Rim belt	Humans in colonies on surface, Gungans in underwater cities	Mostly green, water in underground caves

TIP: **To resize a table and everything in it proportionally** is exactly the same as resizing a graphic: Get the black Selection tool. Hold down the Command and Shift keys (PC: Control and Alt keys), then drag any handle.

Format the text in a table

Formatting the text is exactly the same as formatting text on any InDesign page: Select the text (see the table on page 92 for a reminder on how to select the text) and choose the formatting! When changing the color, select the text and then make sure the **T** is chosen in the Swatches or Color panel.

For now, just choose a font, a size, and a color. We'll do other stuff later.

For clear communication, we want the text in the header (the first row, because we chose to have a header row) to be bolder than the rest, and perhaps in small caps. Your table might look something like the one below.

PLANET	REGION	INHABITANTS	TERRAIN
Tralfamadore	Black Garterbelt	Plumber's friends topped by a hand with a green eye in the palm	Very rocky, with water
K-PAX	D-OXON	Worm-beings, Amps, Rulis, and humanoid Dremers	Cultivated land with many medicinal herbs
Oerth	Greyspace	Dragons and Heroes	Continents, oceans, and islands
Naboo	Mid-Rim belt	Humans in colonies on surface, Gungans in underwater cities	Mostly green, water in underground caves

Format the header

Let's format the header row with a black background fill and white text, as shown on the following page. Follow these instructions carefully.

1 With the Type tool, position the cursor on the left edge of the header row—it turns into a right-pointing arrow.

2 Single-click with the right-pointing arrow to select the row. The row turns black when selected.

3 In the Swatches panel, make sure the Fill box is selected (which it should be, by default). Choose "Black."

4 Now click the **T** in the Swatches panel to change the selection to text; choose the "Paper" color. Click outside the table. It should look like the example on the following page.

Resize columns and rows

To resize any column or row, press-and-drag the column or row dividing line.

1 With the Type tool, press on any column edge, then drag left or right. *Or* press on any row edge, top or bottom, then drag up or down.

2 You'll notice that when you drag a column or row edge, the *columns to the right of* or *the rows below* the one you select move as well.

To resize just your column or row without dragging another column or row along with it, hold down the Shift key and drag the edge. **Try it!**

Planet	Region	Inhabitants	Terrain
Tralfamadore	Black Garterbelt	Plumber's friends topped by a hand with a green eye in the palm	Very rocky, with water
K-PAX	D-OXON	Worm-beings, Amps, Rulis, and humanoid Dremers	Cultivated land with many herbs
Oerth	Greyspace	Dragons and Heroes	Continents, oceans, and islands
Naboo	Mid-Rim belt	Humans in colonies on surface, Gungans in underwater cities	Mostly green, water in underground caves

Standardize the column or row sizes

Sometimes you want some or all the columns to be the same width, or some or all of the rows to be the same height. This is easy to do, although keep in mind it can affect the text flow in the cells.

1 With the Type tool, drag across the columns that you want to standardize or across the rows you want to standardize. You only need to select one cell in each of the columns or rows in order to tell InDesign which columns or rows you want to affect.

For instance, in the example above, select the two cells in the middle of the bottom row. Because these two cells are in two different *columns,* these are the only *columns* that will be affected.

2 Go to the Table menu and choose "Distribute Columns Evenly."

Experiment with distributing rows and columns until you can predict what will happen.

Adjust the text frame

The table doesn't really care whether it is wider or narrow than the text frame, but when the table gets to the bottom of the frame, the last row will disappear if it doesn't have enough room. As usual, you'll see a red plus sign in the Out Port of the frame, as shown below:

At that point, get the black Selection tool and adjust the text frame as you would any text frame—drag the bottom handle down to deepen the frame, or drag it upward to shorten the frame.

To divide up the table and put part of it on another page, treat it just like a text frame (because it is one): With the black Selection tool, shorten the frame, click in the Out Port (shown circled, above), and click on another page to set the rest of the frame.

But let's get back to formatting the table.

Apply color to cells

You probably already know how to change the fill color of a cell: Select the cells with the Type tool (see the chart on page 92 for selection tips) and choose a color from the Color panel or the Swatches panel. Try it on your table—make it look like the one below. Make sure the Fill box is selected before you choose the color.

Planet	Region	Inhabitants	Terrain
Tralfamadore	Black Garterbelt	Plumber's friends topped by a hand with a green eye in the palm	Very rocky, with water
K-PAX	D-OXON	Worm-beings, Amps, Rulis, and humanoid Dremers	Cultivated land with many herbs
Oerth	Greyspace	Dragons and Heroes	Continents, oceans, and islands
Naboo	Mid-Rim belt	Humans in colonies on surface, Gungans in underwater cities	Mostly green, water in underground caves

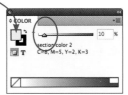

I selected the left-hand column and chose a fill color from the Color panel. I lightened it to 10 percent by dragging the slider (circled, above).

Add rows at the end of a table as you type

If you are entering your data into a table, simply hit the Tab key at the end of the row and it automatically creates a new row with formatting that matches the one it came from.

1 Make sure your text frame is deep enough to hold at least two more rows. If not, use the black Selection tool to drag the window shade handle down a few inches, as you learned in Chapter 2.

2 With the Type tool, click at the end of the text in the last cell.

3 Hit the Tab key. You'll see that a new row is automatically created.

   Fill in the data for this row, as shown below (or make up your own).

4 At the end of that row, hit the Tab key again to start a new row and continue on.

Planet	Region	Inhabitants	Terrain
Tralfamadore	Black Garterbelt	Plumber's friends topped by a hand with a green eye in the palm	Very rocky, with water
K-PAX	D-OXON	Worm-beings, Amps, Rulis, and humanoid Dremers	Cultivated land with many herbs
Oerth	Greyspace	Dragons and Heroes	Continents, oceans, and islands
Naboo	Mid-Rimn belt	Humans in colonies on surface, Gungans in underwater cities	Mostly green, water in underground caves
Arrakis	Ophiuchi C	Bene Gesserit and Fremen	Harsh desert, but it grows spice melange
Fomalhaut	Berenices	Dorsai	Watery world of islands

TIP: **To snap the text frame to the size of the table,** click on the table with the black Selection tool. Go to the Object menu, choose "Fitting," and then choose "Fit Frame to Content." Learn the keyboard shortcut so you can do it easily.

Add rows or columns anywhere in a table

To add a row or column, first click *in the row directly above or below* where you want to insert a new row, or *in a column directly to the left or right* of where you want to insert a new column.

1 With the Type tool, click anywhere in the fourth column.

2 From the Table menu, choose "Insert," and then "Column…."

3 Enter "1" and click the "Right" button. Click OK.

4 Add a new title in the header:

   With the Type tool, click at the end of the word "Terrain."
   Then hit the Tab key to move to the next cell. Type "Moon"
   and it will pick up the formatting in the header.

5 Add the rest of the data: At the end of entering the data into a cell,
   hit the DownArrow key to send the insertion point into the cell
   directly below, ready for typing the next bit of information.
   (To move the insertion point to the next horizontal cell, hit the Tab
   key instead of the DownArrow.)

Planet	Region	Inhabitants	Terrain	Moon
Tralfamadore	Black Garterbelt	Plumber's friends topped by a hand with a green eye in the palm	Very rocky, with water	Pollux
K-PAX	D-OXON	Worm-beings, Amps, Rulis, and humanoid Dremers	Cultivated land with many herbs	No moons, but it orbits two stars, K-MON and K-RIL
Oerth	Greyspace	Dragons and Heroes	Continents, oceans, and islands	Celene and Luna are actually planets in the geosystem
Naboo	Mid-Rim belt	Humans in colonies on surface, Gungans in underwater cities	Mostly green, water in underground caves	Ohma D'un, Rori, and Tasia
Arrakis	Ophiuchi C	Bene Gesserit and Fremen	Harsh desert, but it grows spice melange	Muad'Dib
Fomalhaut	Berenices	Dorsai	Watery world of islands	Albemuth

Delete rows or columns

Select the rows or columns you want to delete (see page 92 about selecting), then press Command Delete (PC: Control Backspace).

Add a pattern of color to rows or columns

When you have many rows or columns, alternating colors can make the information easier to read. InDesign lets you create this effect with the click of a button.

1 With the Type tool, click anywhere in the table.

2 From the Table menu, choose "Table Options," then choose "Alternating Fills…."

   This opens the "Table Options" dialog, as explained on page 94, with the "Fills" pane showing, as shown below.

3 From the "Alternating Pattern" menu, choose "Every Other Row."

   Change "Skip First" to 1 Row.

   Put a check in "Preserve Local Formatting" if you have already colored some cells and don't want them to change. Click OK.

DISCOVERY: Make a copy of your table and experiment with these options for a while! Change the colors, try coloring columns, use a tint, change the number of alternating rows or columns, etc.

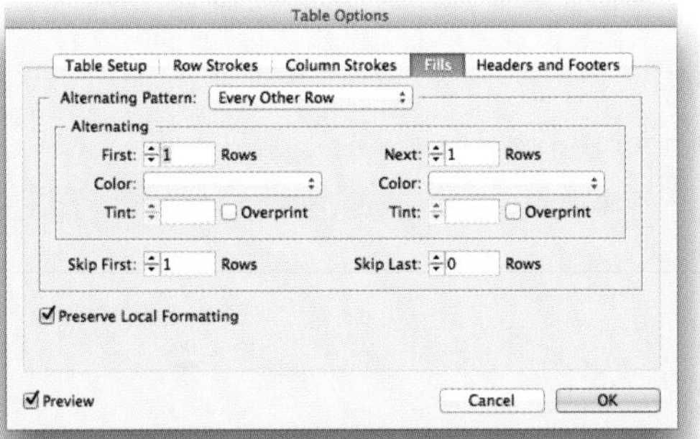

Planet	Region	Inhabitants	Terrain	Moon
Tralfamadore	Black Garterbelt	Plumber's friends topped by a hand with a green eye in the palm	Very rocky, with water	Pollux
K-PAX	D-OXON	Worm-beings, Amps, Rulis, and humanoid Dremers	Cultivated land with many herbs	No moons, but it orbits two stars, K-MON and K-RIL
Oerth	Greyspace	Dragons and Heroes	Continents, oceans, and islands	Celene and Luna are actually planets in the geosystem
Naboo	Mid-Rim belt	Humans in colonies on surface, Gungans in underwater cities	Mostly green, water in underground caves	Ohma D'un, Rori, and Tasia
Arrakis	Ophiuchi C	Bene Gesserit and Fremen	Harsh desert, but it grows spice melange	Muad'Dib
Fomalhaut	Berenices	Dorsai	Watery world of islands	Albemuth

As you continue to add data to the table and come to the end of a row, hit the Tab key to create the next row. It will automatically pick up the fill color in the appropriate rows.

More text formatting

Earlier in this chapter you changed the font, the size, and the color of the type using the standard character formatting. You can also use leading, paragraph spacing, kerning, justification, and everything else you learned in Chapters 2 and 3. But tables have other special formatting you can take advantage of, using the "Cell Options" dialog box that I introduced on page 94.

To change any settings, be sure the insertion point is flashing within the cell that you want to affect, *or* select all the cells to which you want to apply the setting. Then go to the Table menu and choose "Cell Options," and then "Text…."

To create a small space between the cell border and the text, use the "Cell Insets" fields. This moves the text a little away from the border (an example is on page 108). It's an option you'll use regularly. Unclick the chain icon to set different amounts in the fields. **Experiment with this** in the table you created: Select a column and change the "Cell Inset" for the text.

To align text left or right, use the Paragraph panel. **But to align text vertically within the cell,** use "Vertical Justification" in the "Cell Options" dialog box. **Experiment with this** in the table you created: Select a column and change the "Vertical Justification" for the text. For an example, see page 108.

> **TIP:** You can start a table within your text; that is, a table does not have to stand alone. That way the table will move along with the other (non-table) text as you edit. Use the Table Setup dialog box as shown on page 94 to set a "Table Spacing" amount above and below the table, like paragraph spacing.

Customize the strokes

You can customize the strokes or borders around the cells to your heart's content. Make them bold or invisible, dotted or striped, doubled or wavy, any color you like, or even two colors (color the "gap" a different color from the line itself).

Now, *selecting* the exact stroke so you can change it can be a wee bit tricky and crazy-making. Follow these steps to understand how to control them, and then you just have to spend time practicing until you can predict the results. It's worth taking the time now so you won't go crazy later!

1   To practice, create a small table, 4 rows and 4 columns.

2   First, let's put a border around the table:
    With the Type tool, click inside any cell.
    From the Table menu, choose "Table Options," then "Table Setup…."
    Under "Table Border," change the "Weight" to 3 pts. Click OK.

Your table should now look like this.

3   Select two cells in the middle, as shown here:

4   Get the Stroke panel (if it's not on your screen, choose it from the Window menu), shown on the opposite page.

    If your Stroke panel doesn't look like that one, go to its panel menu (click on the tiny hash marks in the upper right of the panel) and choose "Show Options."

    You can also use the settings in the Control panel; they look like this:

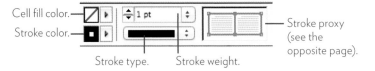

Cell fill color.
Stroke color.
Stroke proxy
(see the
opposite page).
Stroke type.   Stroke weight.

5 In the Stroke panel, you see the formatting for the selected strokes, as shown below. Let's look at these settings carefully.

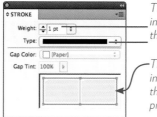

These settings tell me all of the strokes in the selected cells are **1 point** and they are all a **solid black line**.

This is the **proxy**, and it displays the lines that are in the selection in the table. As you can see here, there is an outer border and a vertical line in the proxy, just as there is in the selection.

Any changes you make in the Stroke panel (or changes to the stroke color in the Color or Swatches panel) will apply to the strokes bordering the *selected* cells.

Try it: Change the "Weight" to 2 points and the "Type" to a dotted line. Click anywhere outside the selected cells to see what it looks like.

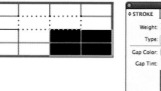

Just what we wanted and expected!

6 The tricky part is when you select a cell that has a custom stroke applied to one or more of its borders. **See what happens:** Select the four bottom corner cells, and look at the Stroke panel again.

The Stroke panel cannot tell us the weight and type of stroke that is applied because the selection includes more than one weight and more than one type.

7 So to change the stroke, you must very carefully **choose the lines in the proxy** that you want to change. In this example, let's change the crossbar strokes in the middle of those four selected cells. **Try it:**

In the proxy, deselect the four lines around the outside (click each one, or double-click one to remove them all).

Select the two crossed lines inside the proxy (click each one, or double-click one to select them both).

Choose a dashed line type and a weight of .5 points.

Ta da! Now practice some more!

Merge and split cells in a table

Tables don't need to consist of only rows and columns like a spreadsheet—you can merge connecting cells to create shapes of all sorts to fit the needs of your data. You might want to merge several cells into one so you can insert a graphic into the space. Try this:

1   Create a new table, as you did on page 104, but make it 5 rows and 3 columns, no header or footer.

2   Select the cells as shown below (press-and-drag over them).

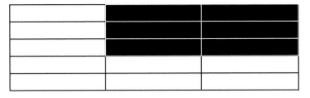

3   From the Table menu, choose "Merge Cells." Those six cells are now one cell.

In the example below, can you see the other place where I merged two cells?

4   By merging cells, you can easily create tables such as this one:

FLEAS

Siphonaptera: Fleas can jump 200 times their body size, which is as if a human jumped about 1200 feet in the air—imagine jumping from the ground and leaping up to the 120th floor of a building.

pablo neruda	ogden nash	jonathan swift
Fleas interest me so much that I let them bite me for hours. They are perfect, ancient, Sanskrit, machines that admit of no appeal. They do not bite to eat, they bite only to jump; they are the dancers of the celestial sphere, delicate acrobats in the softest and most profound circus; let them gallop on my skin, divulge their emotions, amuse themselves with my blood, but someone should introduce them to me. I want to know them closely, I want to know what to rely on.	Adam Had 'em.	So, naturalists observe, a flea Has smaller fleas that on him prey; And these have smaller still to bite 'em, And so proceed *ad infinitum.* Thus ever poet, in his kind, Is bit by him that comes behind.

To insert a graphic, use the Type tool and click in the cell.

From the File menu, choose "Place...."

See Chapter 7 for details on how to move a graphic, crop it, resize it, etc. Everything you learn about graphics will apply to a graphic within a cell.

TIP: Unless you know how large the graphic is, it's a good idea to place the graphic on the page somewhere, resize it to the size you want in the table, then cut the graphic and paste it into the cell.

Use a table instead of tabs and indents

In the previous chapter I mentioned that some designers prefer to use tables instead of tabs. This is an example of where you could use either method, but the table format allows you to colorize columns and structure complex pieces of information quite easily.

If you plan to **use numbers in your table,** be sure to select those columns and give them a flush-right alignment.

To enter the data, use the Tab key to move the text insertion point to the next cell, and use Shift Tab to move it backwards to the left.

The Tab key, as you've probably noticed, does not create tabs—it moves the insertion point to the next cell. **To use a tab setting within a cell,** set it up as usual (using the Tabs panel) and just remember to type Option Tab in the cell when you want to move to a tab marker.

Here you can see the table structure. There is nothing in this table that you don't know how to do.

Double Falsehood by Lewis Theobald

	Prol.	ACT I 1	2	3	ACT II 1	2	3	4	ACT III 1	2	3	ACT IV 1	2	ACT V 1	2	Epil.	TOTAL
Prologue/Epilogue	40	–	–	–	–	–	–	–	–	–	–	–	–	–	–	36	76
Duke Angelo	–	32	–	–	–	–	–	–	–	–	–	–	–	–	75	–	107
his elder son **Roderick**	–	18	–	–	–	–	–	–	–	–	53	44	–	46	49	–	210
his younger son **Henriquez**	–	–	–	51	45	–	47	–	–	41	–	22	–	11	43	–	260
Don Bernard	–	–	31	–	–	–	69	2	–	18	22	–	–	–	9	–	161
his daughter **Leonora** (in love with Julio)	–	–	52	–	–	–	62	32	–	88	–	–	–	17	31	–	282
Camillo	–	–	37	–	–	–	35	–	–	–	50	–	–	–	60	–	182
his son **Julio** (in love with Leonora)	–	–	104	–	–	–	–	–	36	42	–	86	48	–	7	–	323
a maid, **Violante** in love with Henriquez	–	–	–	33	–	39	–	–	–	–	39	40	66	16	29	–	262
Citizen	–	–	–	–	–	–	–	6	12	–	7	–	–	–	–	–	25
Master of the Flocks	–	–	–	–	–	–	–	–	–	–	–	44	–	–	–	–	44
First Shepherd	–	–	–	–	–	–	–	–	–	–	–	25	–	–	–	–	25
Second Shepherd	–	–	–	–	–	–	–	–	–	–	21	–	–	–	–	–	21
														total number of lines			1949

I deleted all the border lines and now it looks so neat and tidy.

Double Falsehood by Lewis Theobald

	Prol.	ACT I 1	2	3	ACT II 1	2	3	4	ACT III 1	2	3	ACT IV 1	2	ACT V 1	2	Epil.	TOTAL
Prologue/Epilogue	40	–	–	–	–	–	–	–	–	–	–	–	–	–	–	36	76
Duke Angelo	–	32	–	–	–	–	–	–	–	–	–	–	–	–	75	–	107
his elder son **Roderick**	–	18	–	–	–	–	–	–	–	–	53	44	–	46	49	–	210
his younger son **Henriquez**	–	–	–	51	45	–	47	–	–	41	–	22	–	11	43	–	260
Don Bernard	–	–	31	–	–	–	69	2	–	18	22	–	–	–	9	–	161
his daughter **Leonora** (in love with Julio)	–	–	52	–	–	–	62	32	–	88	–	–	–	17	31	–	282
Camillo	–	–	37	–	–	–	35	–	–	–	50	–	–	–	60	–	182
his son **Julio** (in love with Leonora)	–	–	104	–	–	–	–	–	36	42	–	86	48	–	7	–	323
a maid, **Violante** in love with Henriquez	–	–	–	33	–	39	–	–	–	–	39	40	66	16	29	–	262
Citizen	–	–	–	–	–	–	–	6	12	–	7	–	–	–	–	–	25
Master of the Flocks	–	–	–	–	–	–	–	–	–	–	–	44	–	–	–	–	44
First Shepherd	–	–	–	–	–	–	–	–	–	–	–	25	–	–	–	–	25
Second Shepherd	–	–	–	–	–	–	–	–	–	–	21	–	–	–	–	–	21
														total number of lines			1949

Try this!

Below is a table that incorporates many of the tasks you completed in this chapter. Can you recreate this—or something like it? Don't forget you can use CreativeCommons.org to find images to use for your project.

I created a table with 7 rows and 4 columns, with no header or footer.

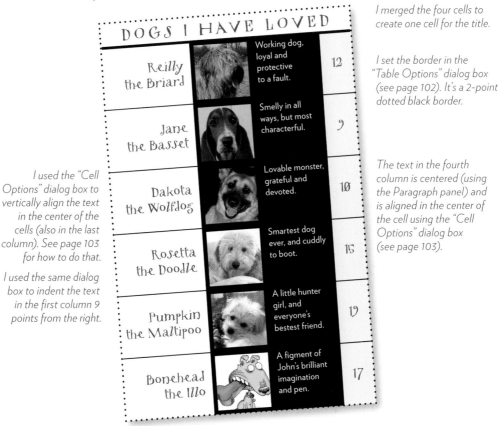

I merged the four cells to create one cell for the title.

I set the border in the "Table Options" dialog box (see page 102). It's a 2-point dotted black border.

I used the "Cell Options" dialog box to vertically align the text in the center of the cells (also in the last column). See page 103 for how to do that.

I used the same dialog box to indent the text in the first column 9 points from the right.

The text in the fourth column is centered (using the Paragraph panel) and is aligned in the center of the cell using the "Cell Options" dialog box (see page 103).

I added a graphic into the cells as explained on page 106.

I sized the graphic frames all to the same size using the Transform panel (page 155) and resized the graphic images inside those frames with the white arrow Direct Selection tool.

I selected the middle two columns and filled them with black.

I filled the fourth column with a tint of another color (see Chapter 8 about tints).

Style Sheets

Style sheets allow you to label, or tag, text with a style name. That style name calls on the style sheet to tell the text exactly what form to take. For instance, you might want all headings in your 24-page brochure to be 18-point Garamond Bold in small caps. So you create the style sheet, or definition, and as you build the brochure, you apply that style sheet (with a click) to all the headings so the formatting just appears as you type. Then your boss tells you, "No, no! The headings must be 16-point Myriad Black." No need to put a hex on your boss—*you merely change the style sheet definition and all the headings that had that style applied will instantly change.*

Style sheets have got to be the most wonderful invention since the computer itself—it's hard to imagine living without them. Even on a one-page document, style sheets can save time and frustration. If you are not using style sheets, you are not tapping into the power of InDesign.

A quick example of paragraph style sheets

Paragraph style sheets apply to entire paragraphs, but remember—every time you hit a Return or the Enter key, you create a paragraph, which means every headline is a paragraph. You can set up paragraph space before and after, hyphenation controls, and all other paragraph settings in a style sheet.

Don't get *style sheets* confused with *type styles.* Type styles are things like bold, italic, underlined, etc.; you will apply type styles within the style sheet definition. Follow the steps below to create and use style sheets!

TASK 1   Create a style sheet for body copy

This will be your "Body copy" style sheet for the main text. In the next task, you will create a Heading style sheet, and then apply it, and in the third task you will change the style sheets to understand why to use them.

1   Open a new, one-page document.

2   Choose the Type tool. Even though there is no text on your page yet, choose a readable font and a type size of 10 or 12 point. Make sure the alignment is flush left. These are now your defaults.

3   Type the text below, hitting Enter or Return at the end of each heading and after the periods you see in the copy.

> Balsamic Vinegar
> Traditional Italian Balsamic vinegar is made from white grapes and is aged in wooden barrels for at least twelve to twenty-five years.
> Apple Cider Vinegar
> Because it is so similar to our stomach acids, apple cider vinegar has been used to ease stomach ailments and actually creates an alkaline reaction in the body.
> Beer Vinegar
> Depending on the type of beer used, this vinegar tends to be sharp and malty.

4   Open the "Paragraph Styles" panel (you can open it from the Type menu if you can't find it on your screen).

5   There are two main ways to make style sheets: From the dialog box, and from type that is already on the page. First, we're going to make a style sheet from type already on the page.

So single-click in the second paragraph, the one that begins with "Traditional Italian Balsamic vinegar is . . . ."

6   In the Paragraph Styles panel, shown below, single-click the *Create new style* icon at the bottom of the panel.

This creates a new style sheet called "Paragraph Style 1."
(If you already have a number of style sheets listed in that panel, you might not see this new one until you scroll through the list.)

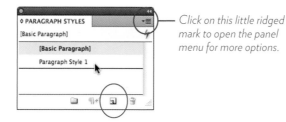

Click on this little ridged mark to open the panel menu for more options.

7   Double-click on "Paragraph Style 1" to open the style sheet specifications dialog box, as shown below.

8   Name this style sheet "Description."

Notice that the style sheet has picked up the formatting from the paragraph in which you had the insertion point flashing.

9   Add an extra point to the "Leading" value, both to open up the linespacing a bit and to make sure it's not using Auto leading.

Use the Tabs pane to move both of the left indent markers about a quarter inch to the right, which will indent the text.

10   Click OK when you're done. Now let's make the Heading style sheet by going straight to the dialog box and choosing attributes (on the following page).

—continued

TASK 2 Create a style sheet for the headings

I assume you completed the previous exercise to create the "Description" style sheet. This new one will be your "Heading" style sheet. If the description copy is a serif typeface, try a bold sans serif for the headings.

1   Open the Paragraph Styles panel, if it isn't already.

2   Choose the black Selection tool and click on a blank spot on the page, just to make sure no text or text frame is selected.

3   Click the "Basic Paragraph" style at the top of the pane.
(The new style sheet picks up the formatting from the selected style sheet. Later you will use this to your advantage.)

From the panel menu, choose "New Paragraph Style...."

You'll get the same dialog box as on the previous page, but this time it's not picking up the formatting of any selected text. It is, however, picking up the formatting of any style sheet in the list that may have been selected, which in this case is "Basic Paragraph." That's okay for now, or click the "Reset to Base" button.

If you see a list of settings in this box that you don't want or don't know what they are, click the button, "Reset to Base."

4   Name this style sheeting "Heading."

5   Select "Basic Character Formats" from the pane on the left; choose a bold sans serif font for the heading.

Choose a font size. (Since sans serifs are generally larger than serif fonts, you probably don't need to make it any larger.)

Select "Indents and Spacing" and add about 8 points of space in the "Space Before" field (as explained in Chapter 4). You can type in 0p8, no matter what the current measurement system it's using.

6   Check the other specs to see what your options are and to make sure there is no unnecessary formatting that you don't want. Click OK.

TASK 3 Apply the style sheets

Now you have two new styles in your Paragraph Styles panel, called "Description" and "Heading." You need to apply them to the text.

1 Select the Type tool.

2 Single-click in the "Balsamic Vinegar" heading.

From the Paragraph Styles panel, single-click on the "Heading" style sheet. It should instantly change to the formatting you selected in Step 2. (If you see a plus sign in the style sheet name, that means there is an override; hold down the Shift and Option/Alt keys and click on the style sheet again. See page 124.)

3 Repeat the above steps to apply the Heading style sheet to the other two vinegar headings.

4 Single-click in the first paragraph of text under the first heading.

From the Paragraph Styles panel, single-click on "Description."

Repeat the above steps to apply the Description style sheet to the other two paragraphs. Your text should look something like this:

Balsamic Vinegar
Traditional Italian Balsamic vinegar is made from white grapes and is aged in wooden barrels for at least twelve to twenty-five years.

Apple Cider Vinegar
Because it is so similar to our stomach acids, apple cider vinegar has been used to ease stomach ailments and actually creates an alkaline reaction in the body.

Beer Vinegar
Depending on the type of beer used, this vinegar tends to be sharp and malty.

Now the best is yet to come. Not only do style sheets help keep your formatting consistent in your document, but they make it incredibly efficient to make changes and fine-tune your typography.

Carry on to the next page!

—continued

TASK 4   Fine-tune the style sheets

This is the part that is so incredibly great about style sheets. Let's say that the short piece you just created is actually a 12-page catalog with hundreds of listings, and your boss tells you to change the color and the size of the heading font throughout the entire document.

All you need to do is change the definition, the formatting specifications, of the style sheet. *Every paragraph to which you had applied that style sheet reformats instantly.*

1   From the Paragraph Styles panel, double-click the "Heading" style sheet name.

2   In the dialog box that opens, change the font, the color, the size, or whatever you want.

3   If the "Preview" box in the bottom-left corner is not checked, check it so you can view the changes.

4   When you're finished making changes, click OK.

5   Follow the steps above to change the formatting for "Description."

Your text should look something like the one below. Your specs are different, of course, but the point is that all the text reformatted when you changed the style sheet definition.

Balsamic Vinegar

Traditional Italian Balsamic vinegar is made from white grapes and is aged in wooden barrels for at least twelve to twenty-five years.

Apple Cider Vinegar

Because it is so similar to our stomach acids, apple cider vinegar has been used to ease stomach ailments and actually creates an alkaline reaction in the body.

Beer Vinegar

Depending on the type of beer used, this vinegar tends to be sharp and malty.

TIP: **To create a new color** while you're in the process of making a new style sheet, Option–double-click (PC: Alt–double-click) on the color box in the upper-left of the Character Color pane.

The basic steps to create style sheets

If you followed the steps on the previous pages, you created style sheets using the two basic methods:

- **Format a paragraph the way you want it to be,** then create the style sheet based on that formatting:

  With the Type tool, click in the formatted paragraph.

  From the Paragraph Styles panel menu, choose "New Paragraph Style...."

  Name the new style, then click OK.

  Apply the style to selected paragraphs.

- **Create a new paragraph style from scratch:**

  From the Paragraph Styles panel menu, choose "New Paragraph Style...."

  Name the new style.

  Select options in the side panel and make your formatting choices.

  When finished, click OK.

  Apply the style to selected paragraphs.

Everything you see in this entire book has style sheets applied, including the graphics (see Chapter 7 about "object styles"). For book-length projects such as this one where every chapter is a different file, InDesign lets me synchronize the style sheets across the files and import individual style sheets from any other InDesign document. When you import a word processing document in which you've used style sheets, InDesign adds those to the Paragraph Styles panel (see pages 126–127 for details about importing Microsoft Word files).

> **TIP:** To end a line but *not* create a new paragraph, use Shift Return or Shift Enter. The line will break, but it won't pick up all the paragraph formatting, such as space before or after, Next Style, etc. This is called a **soft Return.**

Take advantage of "Next Style"

If you're typing your text directly into InDesign, you can take advantage of this great feature where the text automatically becomes a new style after you hit a Return or the Enter key.

For instance, use the text and the style sheet you created on pages 110–114 for the following exercise.

TASK 5   Add a "next style" to the existing style sheets

1   In the Paragraph Styles panel, double-click on the "Heading" style sheet you made earlier.

2   In the "General" pane that appears, find the "Next Style" pop-up menu; choose the "Description" style sheet you created earlier.

Click OK.

3   In the Paragraph Styles panel, double-click on the "Description" style.

4   In the "General" pane that appears, from the "Next Style" pop-up menu, choose the "Heading" style sheet.

Click OK.

TASK 6   Continue typing in the text

1   Get the text sample that you created earlier.

With the black Selection tool, enlarge the size of the text frame so it will easily hold more type.

2   Get the Type tool.

Click at the end of the last paragraph in that text frame.

3   Hit Enter or Return and type a new heading. It should be automatically formatted in the "Heading" style sheet!

4   At the end of the heading, hit Enter or Return and type a description. The text should appear in the "Description" formatting.

Hit Enter or Return at the end of the description text and type a new heading, repeating the process over and over.

The trick to using "Next Style," obviously, is that you have to have the style sheets created so you can choose them.

TIP: Choosing a "Next Style" does *not* change any text that is already on the page—it only applies as you're in the process of typing.

Here is another example of when the "Next Style" feature is useful. Let's say you're working on a newsletter and as you enter the text, you typically type a subhead, hit Enter, type the first paragraph which does *not* have an indent (because first paragraphs should not be indented), then you type the next paragraph which *does* have an indent. That makes three style sheets: one for the Subhead, one for the First Paragraph, and one for the Body Copy.

TASK 7   Try another example of using "Next Style"

1   Create the Body Copy style sheet and include an indent (use either the "Indents and Spacing" pane or the "Tabs" pane for the indent). For "Next Style," choose "Same Style." Click OK.

2   In the Paragraph Styles panel, single-click to select "Body Copy," then from the panel menu, choose "New Paragraph Style…."

3   Name this "Body Copy First Paragraph."

Because "Body Copy" was chosen in the panel before you made this new style, this new style *is automatically based on* "Body Copy" and holds all the same formatting.

So in this new style sheet, delete the indent, which will be the only difference from "Body Copy."

From the "Next Style" pop-up menu, choose "Body Copy." Click OK.

4   Create a new style sheet, and name this one "Subhead."

From the "Based on" pop-up menu, choose "No paragraph style."

Format it as you wish, perhaps a bold sans serif.

From the "Next Style" pop-up menu, choose "Body Copy First Paragraph." Click OK.

TASK 8   Now type the text

1   Create a new text frame.

2   Choose the paragraph style called "Subhead"; type a short subhead and hit Enter or Return.

3   Type the first paragraph—notice the style changed and it is now "Body Copy First Paragraph"; hit Enter or Return.

4   Type the next couple of paragraphs—notice the style automatically changed to "Body Copy." The Body Copy text will continue in the same style until you manually choose another.

Be careful with the "Based On" feature!

The option to base one style sheet on another can be great, as long as you are clear about what will happen. The basic idea is this: Let's say you have a newsletter. For the body copy, you create a Body Copy style sheet that uses Garamond Regular, 11/14. For the captions, you create a Captions style sheet that is *based on* the Body Copy style sheet, but it uses Garamond Italic, 9/10. For the headlines, you create a Headlines style sheet that is *based on* the Body Copy style sheet, but it uses Garamond Bold 13/18.

Now let's say your client tells you she doesn't want to use Garamond; she wants you to change the font to Minion. All you need to do is change Body Copy to Minion Regular—the other styles that are based on Body Copy will change as well. The Captions will automatically change to Minion Italic and the Headlines to Minion Bold. They will maintain the specifications you set up that were different; that is, the Captions will still be 9/10 and the Headlines will still be 13/18. This is great!

The problem arises when you don't realize that you based StyleB on StyleA, or you didn't know what you were doing or you forget that you did that. Then when you change StyleA, you're surprised when StyleB changes as well!

It is safest to only base one style on another when you are really clear about exactly why you are doing it and what the consequences might be. At any time, of course, you can change StyleB so it is no longer based on StyleA, but that's a painful waste of time. Although, it will teach you not to do it again.

TASK 9   Base one style on another

1   In the Paragraph Styles panel, create a new style (as explained on page 115 or pages 110–112).

Make sure the new style is not based on any style: In the "Based On" pop-up menu in the panel, choose "No paragraph style." You might also want to click the "Reset to Base" button to get rid of any previous formatting.

Name this style "Headline," and make it something like Calibri Bold (a sans serif), 18-point text with 20-point leading. Click OK.

2   In the Paragraph Styles panel, single-click on your new style, "Headline." From the panel menu, choose "New Paragraph Style."

Call this one "Subhead." Notice it is already based on "Headline" because that is the style you had selected when you chose to make a new style.

Change the font size to 12 point, the leading value to 14, and make it Calibri Regular. Click OK.

3 If you still have the "Body copy" style sheet you created on page 96, skip to Step 4; if not, make a quick "Body copy" style sheet.

4 Okay. Now create a text frame and type something like the piece shown below, left.

5 When finished, open the "Headline" style sheet. Change the font to a serif face, such as Garamond or Georgia. Also change the color to something noticeable, such as bright blue or red. Click OK.

6 Your sample should have changed similar to the one below, right. The Body copy should not change because it was not based on the Headline, but the Subheads should reflect the font and color changes.

Can you imagine how this could mess up your entire project if you randomly base style sheets on other style sheets?

Mosaic Tiles

There is a wide variety of mosaic tiles available for creating projects galore. Explore the possibilities with the set provided in this special box.

Smalti

Smalti is the handmade glass used in the mosaics of medieval and Renaissance Europe. Molten glass is poured onto a slab for cooling, and then cut by hand into tiny, irregular pieces. The colors never fade.

Pebbles

Pebble mosaics are especially useful in high traffic areas, such as in parks, on walkways, or even in a busy, urban street.

Millefiori

Millefiori are tiny, round, ornamental glass pieces cut from glass rods of fused colors. Use them to create patterns amongst a field of plainer tiles.

The Subheads are *based on* the Headline style sheet.

Mosaic Tiles

There is a wide variety of mosaic tiles available for creating projects galore. Explore the possibilities with the set provided in this special box.

Smalti

Smalti is the handmade glass used in the mosaics of medieval and Renaissance Europe. Molten glass is poured onto a slab for cooling, and then cut by hand into tiny, irregular pieces. The colors never fade.

Pebbles

Pebble mosaics are especially useful in high traffic areas, such as in parks, on walkways, or even in a busy, urban street.

Millefiori

Millefiori are tiny, round, ornamental glass pieces cut from glass rods of fused colors. Use them to create patterns amongst a field of plainer tiles.

So when you change the Headline style sheet, all styles *based on* Headline change as well.

Create and use character styles

Character styles function in exactly the same way as paragraph styles, except they apply only to *selected characters,* not to the entire paragraph. You can choose basic text formatting, such as font, style, size, color, kerning or tracking values, and more.

Just like paragraph styles, once you have applied the styles to text, you can change the style sheet definition and all instances of that character style throughout the document will change. It's miraculous. You've seen a lot of character styles throughout this book—the numbers of the steps in the tasks, the bullets, the task headings, etc. The bold sans serif that begins the paragraph above is a character style—all I did was select the text, then click the name of the style and voilà, the formatting changed. If I want to make all those bold words in this whole chapter a bright pink color, all it would take is a click in the style sheet definition.

TASK 10 Create a character style

1 Open the Characters Styles panel.

2 From the panel menu, choose "New Character Style…."

3 Name the style something that will tell you what it will be used for.

4 Make sure "Based On" is "None" (for this example, anyway).

5 Click each of the options in the side pane and make your formatting choices. *You don't have to make a choice for every item*—you might only have one or two formatting specifications. Anything you leave blank will be picked up by the paragraph formatting.

   For instance, perhaps you want to highlight words in your report in bold magenta. In your character style, only change the "Font Style" to Bold and the "Character Color" to magenta. Do that for this task, and click OK.

TASK 11 Apply a character style

1 Select text in a paragraph.

2 Click the style name you just created. That's it!

   To remove any character style, select the formatted text, go to the Character Styles panel, and choose "None."

Oh boy—nested styles!

Nested styles are really amazing. Once you make a character style or two, you can set up a paragraph style that automatically applies a character style at certain points. For instance, when I type a task heading, as on the opposite page, the first words automatically appear in a tint of the blue color and in small caps; when I hit the Tab key, the formatting automatically changes to the paragraph style sheet.

You're not limited to using only one character style—you can use many, surely more than you'll ever want to use in one paragraph.

If you're feeling confident in your ability to create style sheets that include tabs, indents, spacing, etc., let's create a nested style that creates the format shown below; it is created automatically as you type.

SUNDAY   *Sun's Day: The Sun is personified as a goddess.*

TASK 12 Create a nested style sheet

1 First, you need to create a **character style sheet.**

   Create one new character style sheet called "Red Day." Make it a sans serif bold font, 9 point, 10.2 leading, small caps. Choose a color of your choice (if you know how to create colors, as explained in Chapter 11, double-click on the color swatch in the "Character Color" section to create a new swatch).

2 Now create the **paragraph style sheet.**

   Name it "Days of week." Choose a serif font, 10/12, left alignment, paragraph "Space After" of 0p4 (in the "Indents and Spacing" pane, as on page 112). Set the left indent marker at 5 picas, as shown below.

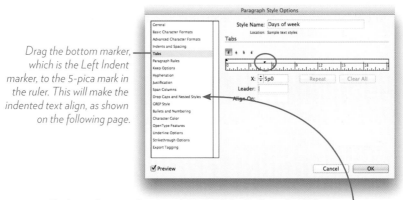

Drag the bottom marker, which is the Left Indent marker, to the 5-pica mark in the ruler. This will make the indented text align, as shown on the following page.

3 Click on "Drop Caps and Nested Styles" in the left pane.

—continued

121

4   Click the button, "New Nested Style."

This puts a pop-up menu in the "Nested Styles" pane, as shown below. Click on it to choose your character style named "Red Day."

Recreate the settings you see below ("through 1" and "Tab Characters"). This tells the style sheet to use that character style *until* you hit the first Tab key. Click OK.

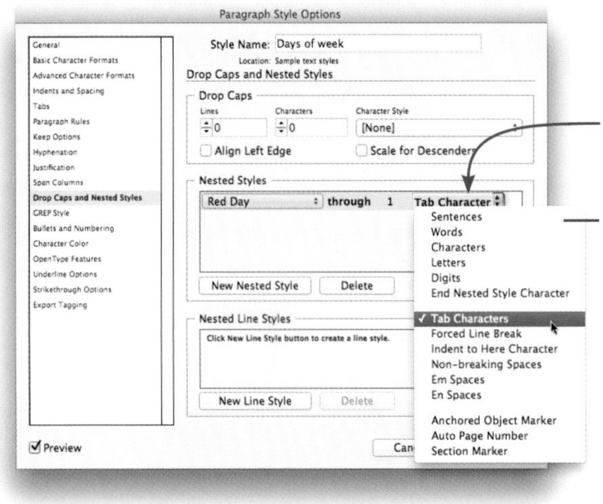

Click in this field to make the menu arrows appear.

Spend a couple of minutes perusing this list of options. The character style will appear until you type one or more of these items. The item itself will be included in the character style depending on whether you choose "through" or "up to."

5   Create a text frame and choose the paragraph style, "Days of week."

Type the list below, typing the day of the week in all lowercase (the intro paragraph, obviously, has a different paragraph style!). Hit a Tab after the name of each day. Ta da!

The English days of the week preserve the original pagan associations (except Saturday, which is of Roman origin).

SUNDAY	*Sun's Day: The Sun is personified as a goddess.*
MONDAY	*Moon's Day: The Moon is personified as a god.*
TUESDAY	*Tiw's Day: Tiw, or Tyr, is a Norse god similar to Mars, the Roman god of war.*
WEDNESDAY	*Woden's Day: Woden, or Odin, is a Norse psychopomp.*
THURSDAY	*Thor's Day: Thor is the god of thunder.*
FRIDAY	*Frige's Day: Frige is an Anglo-Saxon love goddess.*
SATURDAY	*Saturn's day: Named after the Roman god Saturn, god of agriculture and harvest.*

The left indent marker you set at 5 picas (in Step 2) is what makes the text line up at this point.

6 If you're feeling sassy, **create a second character style** called "Blue Deity." Make it the same sans serif, bold, 9/10.2. Choose (or create and choose) a teal color.

Add it to the same paragraph style, "Days of week."

Make the second character style begin after you type a colon.

All the text with that paragraph style applied will automatically change. Amazing.

The English days of the week preserve the original pagan associations (except Saturday, which is of Roman origin).

SUNDAY	Sun's Day: *The Sun is personified as a goddess.*
MONDAY	Moon's Day: *The Moon is personified as a god.*
TUESDAY	Tiw's Day: *Tiw, or Tyr, is a Norse god similar to Mars, the Roman god of war.*
WEDNESDAY	Woden's Day: *Woden, or Odin, is a Norse psychopomp.*
THURSDAY	Thor's Day: *Thor is the god of thunder.*
FRIDAY	Frige's Day: *Frige is an Anglo-Saxon love goddess.*
SATURDAY	Saturn's day: *Named after the Roman god Saturn, god of agriculture and harvest.*

Here are some other tips about the nested styles and drop caps.

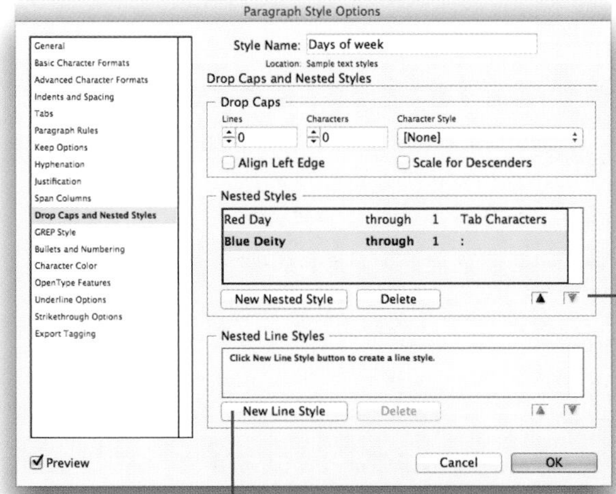

Experiment with the Drop Caps feature. It creates a large initial cap, as shown here. **To apply a drop cap to a single paragraph** instead of to the paragraph style, click in a paragraph and then choose "Drop Caps and Nested Styles" from the Paragraph panel menu.

To move a nested character style up or down in the appearance order, select it, then click one of these buttons.

To make a character style appear for a certain number of entire lines, add it here and choose the number of lines.

Know your overrides

Even though you've applied style sheets to just about everything, you can still change selected characters. For instance, this paragraph you're reading has a "Body copy" style applied, but *I can make selected characters italic.* This is called an **override,** where I override the basic settings. You can override everything. InDesign considers a character style, such as the bold in the previous sentence, also an override, but recognizes it is a character style.

When you select an entire paragraph (triple-click in it) and see a **+** sign in the style name in the panel, as shown below, that means there is at least one override in that paragraph. Sometimes you don't know even how they got there.

There are many ways to get rid of overrides, depending on what they are and what you want to do, but I'm just going to mention the two most useful. Check the Adobe Help files for all the complex ways of clearing local formatting!

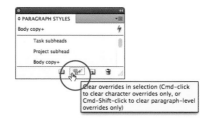

Hover over a style sheet that displays a **+** sign, and a tool tip appears to tell you what the override is and how to clear it.

When a paragraph is selected that has overrides in it, the *Clear Override* button is available. Hover to read its message.

Keyboard shortcuts to remove overrides: With the Type tool, single-click in a paragraph, or press-and-drag to select more than one.

	Mac	Windows
Clear local formatting such as words that you changed to italic with a keyboard shortcut	*Option-click the style name*	*Alt-click the style name*
Clear local formatting and character styles	*Shift-Option-click the style name*	*Shift-Alt-click the style name*

DISCOVERY: Also experiment with contextual menus—right-click on a selected style name in the panel to see what your options are!

Tips for style sheets

Here are some tips that make using style sheets even easier:

- **Give the style sheet a name that tells you what it does.** That is, don't randomly name them things like Body 1 and Body 2, or New Headline and Newer Headline. Be specific so you know exactly what you'll be getting.

- **Name the styles in related groups.** For instance, if you have a quiz included in your handouts document, name the style sheets pertinent to that portion, something like Quiz Headings, Quiz Questions, Quiz Answers, etc. This way you can group them together in the panel so you can find them easily.

- **Assign keyboard shortcuts** to the styles you use the most: In the Style Options for either paragraph or characters styles, go to the "General" pane and click in the "Shortcut" field. Hold down the Command, Option, or Shift key (PC: Control, Alt, or Shift), then tap a number *on the numeric keypad.* You must use the numeric keypad for this—if your keyboard doesn't have one, you can't create a shortcut. Dang.

    If you hear a beep when you try to type the shortcut, that means your Num Lock is not on. Cancel the dialog box, and turn on Num Lock (even if you don't have a Num Lock key, the Clear key usually acts as one). Try again.

- **When placing or pasting text,** choose a style sheet *before* placing or pasting, and the text will appear on the page in that style. This is a particularly great feature.

- If you start typing with a style sheet and the **text appears in completely different formatting** from what you specified, it somehow grabbed some overrides. To fix this, use the keyboard shortcut on the opposite page to "Clear local formatting and character styles." Also, click in an empty spot (not in a text frame) and then clear the overrides when nothing is selected; this prevents the problem from happening again.

> **TIP:** At any point you can **remove the style sheet from the text** without removing the formatting. Select the text, go to the panel menu, and choose "Break Link to Style."

Import style sheets along with a Word doc

If you use Microsoft Word, either you know how to use your style sheets, or you just type away and style sheets (some that include settings such as "Next Style") are automatically applied for you (which I find *really* annoying).

When you place a Word doc into InDesign, the default is set so Word's style sheets are added to your Paragraph Styles panel. You'll know they're there because the panel displays old-fashioned floppy disk icons next to each imported style sheet name, as shown below.

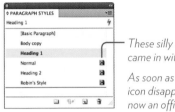

These silly icons tell you these styles came in with the file you imported.

As soon as you edit a style sheet, this icon disappears, indicating the style is now an official InDesign style sheet.

Imported style sheets in InDesign

If a style sheet in Word **is named exactly the same** as a style sheet in your InDesign file, InDesign's style takes over. For instance, the panel you see above included a style sheet named "Heading 1," so when the Word style sheet was imported along with the text, my InDesign style sheet applied its settings to every paragraph tagged with "Heading 1." This is great for me. :-)

Any style sheets in the Word doc that don't find the exact name in the panel are imported and *added* to your panel. This is also great because it doesn't really matter what the original formatting was—once it is tagged and in InDesign, you can format the entire document so easily.

More control over importing style sheets

Occasionally, however, someone has monkeyed with the defaults and weird things happen when you import a Word file, or perhaps the defaults simply don't do just what you want. For instance, you might have spent a lot of time in Word creating exactly the style sheets you need for this project, and you want to make sure those don't get overridden when you import the file to InDesign. In that case, follow the steps below.

Customize the import and map the style sheets

1 In the InDesign file, go to the File menu and choose "Place…."

2 Check the box in the lower-left of the Place window to "Show Import Options."

3 Find and double-click the Word document that you want to import.

4 In the "Microsoft Word Import Options" dialog box that appears, carefully read the options and make decisions about the incoming file.

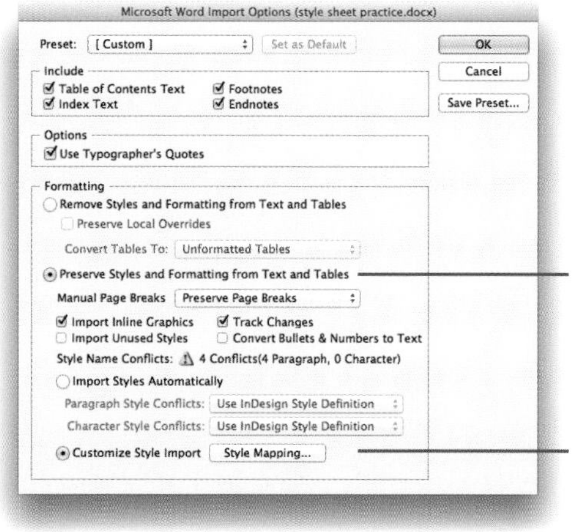

This is the standard default.

Click here to remap the incoming styles.

5 Click "Customized Style Import," and then click "Style Mapping…."

In the "Style Mapping" dialog box that appears (shown below), click on the InDesign style on the right that matches up with the Word style; this pops up a menu.

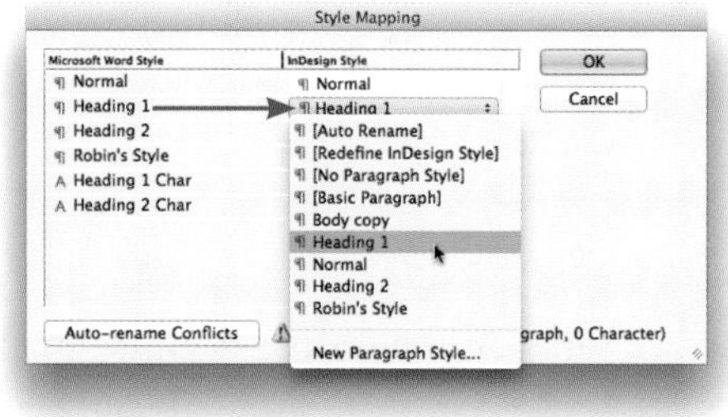

To maintain the imported Word style, choose "Redefine InDesign Style." This forces the InDesign's style sheet to reformat itself according to the Word style.

To format the imported style sheet with the InDesign style, choose an existing InDesign style.

To rename the Word style, choose "Auto Rename."

6 To close the "Style Mapping" dialog box, click OK, and then click OK in the main dialog box (far above) to finish importing the file.

Try This!

Where style sheets really shine is in longer documents (although I end up using style sheets on *everything*). Recreate the project you see below, using style sheets for each different formatting.

A handy resource for lots of copyright-free text to work with is:

http://www.gutenberg.org/browse/scores/top

Just choose a story on the Gutenberg site (with grateful appreciation), copy a bunch of text, and add your own headlines and subheads to divide it into sections. Take advantage of everything you have learned about tabs and indents, leading, paragraph spacing, kerning, etc.

The text in the project below is from *How to Analyze People on Sight Through the Science of Human Analysis: The Five Human Types,* 1921, by Elsie Lincoln Benedict, available on the Gutenberg site (I did a little editing on the text below).

play with **graphics** and COLOR in INDESIGN

Of course, everyone's favorite is color and graphics—so much sexier than text. And InDesign has lots to offer in this area. In fact, as packed as this section is with things to do, there is more that just couldn't fit in. But I hope you take some of these techniques and ideas and really explore the possibilities beyond these pages!

A man who works with

his hands is a laborer;

a man who works with

his hands and his brain

is a craftsman.

But a man who works

with his hands

and his brain

and his heart

is an artist.

Louis Nizer, attorney and artist, 1902–1994

7 All About Graphics

Well, certainly not *all* about graphics, but enough to get you started and keep you busy for a while.

InDesign has added more and more graphic capabilities to its page layout features. If you are an Illustrator user, you'll find the drawing tools are very similar, though more limited. If you are a Photoshop user, you'll be pleased to see how quickly you can pop into Photoshop from InDesign to adjust your images. And if you've never used any of Adobe's Creative Suite before, you will be astounded at what you can do with your unleashed creativity.

Graphic formats

The short story: Use PDF, **.ai**, **.psd**, or **.tif** for graphics to be printed (although you can get away with .jpg files on your small desktop printer). **Scan images** as TIFFS. You can actually place another InDesign file onto an InDesign page.

Avoid PICT, WMF, BMP, PNG, and only use EPS and DCS if you know what you're doing and have no choice.

Vector files from Illustrator

When saving an .ai file in Illustrator, make sure the box is checked to "Create PDF Compatible File" in the options when you save the file or InDesign won't be able to read it. Avoid EPS files, if you can, only because they are an old technology and not as dependable as .ai files.

Graphic color

When you view graphics on your computer screen, they are displayed in **RGB (red, green, blue) mode**. Graphics that have been commercially printed—like those in this book, in any magazine, or on your cereal box—were created in **CMYK (cyan, magenta, yellow, black) mode**.

These two modes are not interchangeable. Most commercial printers cannot accurately print an RGB image, and what you see on screen *is not* what you'll get in your printed project.

So, when you are creating a graphic that is to be viewed on a screen, like a new logo for your web site, you'll want that image to be in RGB mode. Anything you're going to have printed by a commercial printer should be in CMYK.

Many home and office printers print in RGB. However, if your printer takes *four* (or more) separate color cartridges, you will usually get better results if you work in CMYK. See Chapter 8 on Color for more details.

Graphic resolution

Photographs and Photoshop graphics are **raster** images; they are comprised of a fixed number of pixels and are measured in pixels per inch (ppi). A *high-resolution* image, say 300 ppi, is one that contains enough pixels to *resolve* the image clearly. The image resolution is determined by the original source file; that is, if the photo is from your old cell phone, it's pretty low-res and there's not much you can do about it (well, John has some great tips in our book, *The Non-Designer's Photoshop Book;* see the image of Scarlett on page 159 of this book for an example of a low-res image made beautiful).

Generally, for commercial printing use 300 ppi images; desktop printing on an inexpensive inkjet printer is of pretty low quality anyway, so low-res photos don't look much worse than anything else.

However, when you reduce the size of a bitmap image on the page in InDesign, you effectively increase its ppi—the pixels in the image become smaller and so they *appear* to be better resolved. This lets you cheat on some images, although they still won't have as much detail. InDesign's Links panel keeps track of an image's actual ppi and its effective ppi; see page 160.

*The cropped image above has an **actual ppi** of 72 and is placed on the page at 100 percent size, so its **effective ppi** is also 72.*

Reducing the same image to 25 percent reduced its effective ppi to 288, legitimately printable. But you can see that even though it is not as pixelated, there is still a lack of detail.

The display performance

Even if your graphics are high resolution, they might appear to be low resolution on the InDesign page, depending on the "Display Performance" settings in the preferences. Go to the Preferences dialog box (from the InDesign menu on a Mac; from the File menu on a PC), where you can **set a document default** so all your graphics display either "Fast," "Typical," or "High Quality." **To set an application default** for all new documents that you create, choose a display option before you open any document.

The advantage of a "Fast" display is that if you have an old and slow machine, the images are all gray boxes and so your pages load very fast and you can move the graphics around quickly—but you can't see the images. A "Typical" display shows a lower resolution image, again for faster working time, and "High Quality," of course, shows your best high-quality image.

You can **override the default** for individual graphics: Select one or more images, then right-click to get the contextual menu shown below.

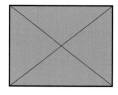

This is what images look like when you choose a "Fast Display" performance.

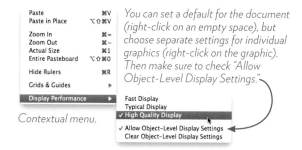

Contextual menu.

You can set a default for the document (right-click on an empty space), but choose separate settings for individual graphics (right-click on the graphic). Then make sure to check "Allow Object-Level Display Settings."

Drawn Graphics

There is a lot you can do with graphics that you draw right on the page in InDesign. You can make quick and easy shapes to use as lively frames and backgrounds for text or to enhance other images you draw or import. If you actually know how to draw, take advantage of the Pen and Pencil tools.

More importantly, all the things you can do to the frames and fills and strokes in drawn graphics, you can do to text and graphic frames. So don't skip this section just because you don't think you'll be using drawing tools for illustration!

All graphics drawn on the page in InDesign are in the vector format so you can enlarge them as much as you want and they will always print nice and crisp.

The line and shape tools

You have probably used shape tools before, and InDesign's work the same as any other: **Get the tool, press-and-drag on the page.** Every shape has a **frame,** whether you can see it or not. You can change the stroke and the fill, as explained on page 136. To reshape a drawn shape, see pages 138–139. **Do these easy tasks:**

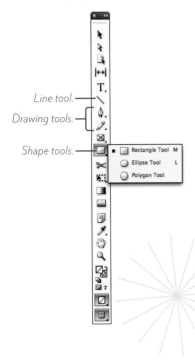

Line tool.

Drawing tools.

Shape tools.

To constrain proportions to a perfect square or circle, hold the Shift key while dragging.

To start a shape from its center instead of its corner, hold the Option (PC: Alt key) while dragging.

To move a shape before letting go, hold down the Spacebar and drag to another position.

Rectangle and Ellipse tools: *Click* on the page (instead of press-and-drag) to get a dialog box where you can enter a specific size.

Polygon tool: *Click* on the page (instead of press-and-drag) to get a dialog box where you can enter a height and width, and also the number of sides and how deeply they are inset (which makes points). An inset of zero prevents a star shape; an inset of 100 percent gives you straight lines connected in the middle. Try it!

Double-click on the Polygon tool icon in the Tools panel to set just the sides and inset.

The Polygon tool is crazy wild

I'm not quite sure how useful this is, but the Polygon tool can do things no other tool can do. First experiment with it by using the techniques explained at the bottom of the opposite page. InDesign retains the settings for the next polygon you draw. When you're comfortable creating them, try these tasks.

TASK 1 Go insane with the Polygon tool

- **Reshape a drawn polygon:** With the black Selection tool, select the shape. Double-click on the Polygon tool icon in the Tools panel and enter new specs.

- **Reshape the polygon as you create it:** Drag out a polygon, but don't let go of the mouse or trackpad button. Tap the Spacebar once (nothing appears to happen), then use the arrow keys. The UpArrow and DownArrow increase and decrease the number of sides; the LeftArrow and RightArrow increase and decrease the inset.

  If you're feeling confident, use this technique combined with the next two, below.

- **Multiply the polygons:** Draw a polygon, but don't let go of the mouse or trackpad button; tap the UpArrow key. Each time you tap, another polygon appears, *above* the first one; tap the DownArrow key to delete a polygon. Since your button is still down, drag to resize all of those polygons at once.

- **Make a grid of polygons:** Follow the steps above to multiply the polygons. When you've got a nice tall column of them, tap the RightArrow key to make a new column. Drag to the right and simultaneously tap the RightArrow key to create a whole darn grid. To delete a column, tap the LeftArrow key.

- Use the technique mentioned on the opposite page to **move the polygon** before you're finished: Hold down the Spacebar and drag the entire collection.

- When you let go of the collection of polygons, they are automatically all selected. This would be a great time to group them together (see page 140) or change their fills and strokes, as explained on the following page.

- Also see page 139 to alter individual points, sides, or insets on any polygon.

- Also see page 138 to add corner options to polygons!

Strokes and fills

Every frame has a **stroke** around it (a border), whether or not you can see it. And the inside has a **fill** color. A frame can have a fill and at the same time have content, such as an image (in which case it is a graphic frame) or text (in which case it is a text frame). The three frames (shape, image, and text) are each a little different from each other, but all can have strokes and fills.

TASK 2   Change the fill and stroke of a shape

The trick to changing a stroke or a fill is to **first select these three things:**

- Select the *object* with the black Selection tool.
- Select the *Container Formatting box* in the Swatches panel, as shown below (if you selected a shape frame, this box is already chosen; get in the habit of checking anyway).
- Select the *Fill* or *Stroke* box in the Swatches panel, as shown below.

Container Formatting box. Text Formatting box.

Fill box.
Stroke box.

Learn all about creating more colors in Chapter 8.

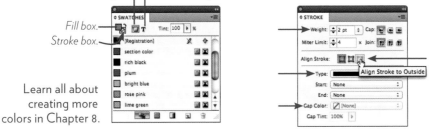

1   Select and change the **fill:** Make sure you have selected the three items listed above (including the Fill box), then choose your color.

2   Select and change the **stroke:** Make sure you have selected the three items listed above (including the Stroke box), then:

- Choose your stroke color from the Swatches panel.
- From the Stroke panel, choose a "Weight" and a "Type."
- If you choose any stroke besides the solid one, you can also choose a color for the **gap** between the lines. Try it! Don't be a wimp— play with the possibilities of giant wavy strokes or dots!
- Be aware that the "Align Stroke" options change the size of your shape. Below, all the boxes are the same size, with a 3-point stroke.

No stroke.   *Aligned to center.*   *Aligned to inside.*   *Aligned to outside.*

Manipulating the shapes

Knowing how to manipulate the shapes and frames and fills is important because, as I mentioned before, these techniques apply to all frames in InDesign—drawn shapes, placed graphics, and text.

TASK 3   Resize an object

Resizing a *shape* (not a frame with an *image* in it; see pages 148–149 for that) is the same as in many other programs you may have used. Essentially, you are resizing the frame itself in this operation, but since a shape frame has no content (just a fill), it works to resize the shape.

1   With the black Selection tool, drag any handle.

2   **To maintain the same proportion,** hold down the Shift key and drag.
    To resize from the center outwards, press on the handle, and then hold down the Option key (PC: Alt key) and drag.

TASK 4   Copy an object

1   Get the black Selection tool.

2   Hold down the Option key (PC: Alt key), then press-and-drag the object.
    To drag the object perfectly horizontally or vertically, hold down the Shift key as well as the Option key.

TASK 5   Rotate an object

1   With the black Selection tool, single-click the image.

2   Position the pointer just outside any corner handle—you'll see the curved double-arrow appear. At that point, press-and-drag to rotate the object.

    Or select the object, then choose the Rotate tool from the Tools panel. Position the rotate cursor (which looks like crosshairs) anywhere on the page and drag.

    Or enter a rotation amount in the *Rotation Angle* field in the Transform panel (see page 155).

    To put the image back into its normal rotation, select the graphic with the black Selection tool. Right-click on the P icon in the Control panel; this pops up a contextual menu with one option, to "Clear Transformations." *Or* select the object, go to the Transform panel (page 155), and from its panel menu choose "Clear Transformations."
    Or enter zero in the *Rotation Angle* field in the Transform panel.

TASK 6 Use the Corner Options

You have a choice of several corner options for any frame. They're not terribly useful, but it's good to know they're there. Sometimes you might want to take the harsh edge off the corners, or add a bit of a fancy one on a text frame for a special invitation. If you combine a shaped corner with a fancy stroke with a gap color, you can create some interesting effects.

1　With the black Selection tool, select the frame (try this on a shape or graphic frame for now).

2　From the Object menu, choose "Corner Options...."

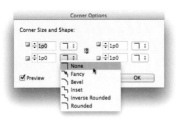

To change each corner individually, click the **chain link icon** so it is unlocked. If you want all the corners the same, make sure the chain is locked.

To change a corner, choose a corner style from the pop-up menu. If the square corner is chosen, that means no style is applied.

3　You can see the changes on your frame as you enter values in these corner fields. Click OK when finished.

To remove all corner styles, make sure the chain icon is locked, then choose the square corner from any pop-up menu, as shown above.

This image uses "Inverse Rounded" corners, 0p10, with a 3-point Thick-Thin stroke with a gap color of Paper.

Try this for fun!

The crazy shapes below are actually polygons that have had their corners reshaped with the "Corner Options" dialog box (above) and various strokes applied with colored gaps. The first three are groups of two polygons each; I used the Smart Guides to center the small shapes within the larger shapes.

TASK 7   Use the Live Corners controls

If you haven't turned off the **Live Corners control,** you see a little yellow box on the upper-right edge of most frames. This control lets you adjust corners directly on the frame, and you can adjust them individually.

To hide or show this control, go to the View menu, choose "Extras," and then choose to "Hide [or Show] Live Corners." (Since you'll use it so rarely, I recommend turning the control off until you need it.)

1   Click the yellow Live Corner control; all four corners now have a yellow diamond-shaped control.

2   **To reshape all the corners the same,** drag any yellow diamond.

3   **To reshape just one corner,** hold down the Shift key and drag.

4   **To change the corner shapes** to any of those listed in the dialog box on the opposite page, hold down the Option key (PC: Alt key) and click on any yellow diamond. Continue to hold down the key and click to cycle through the options.

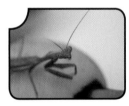

I held down both the Shift key and the Option/Alt key to change just the one corner in the upper-left.

I held down the Shift key to change the other corners individually.

TASK 8   Reshape an object

There are many opportunities in design for altering the shape of a frame, and there are several ways to do it in InDesign. Try these:

1   With the black Selection tool, select a frame of any sort.

2   Double-click on the Polygon tool in the Tools panel.

3   Set the number of sides and the inset, then click OK. Voilà.

Also try this more useful technique

1   With the white Direct Selection tool, single-click on any object.

2   Then with the same tool, single-click directly on the frame so you see the individual white points. They are really tiny, so it's hard to see them. Watch the cursor—you'll see a tiny square when you are positioned over a point.

3   Press-and-drag on that point. Do the same to any other point that you wish to reshape.

TASK 9   Group elements together

You can group as many objects together as you like, and then apply settings to all of them at once, or move them all, delete them, resize them, etc.

1   Draw a number of shapes on the page.

2   With the black Selection tool, do one of the following:

- **To select more than one object,** hold down the Command key (PC: Control key) and single-click on various items. Each one you click becomes part of the group.
  To deselect an object from the group, Command-click (PC: Control-click) on that individual item.

- *Or* with the black Selection tool, **press** on an empty spot outside of any shape, **then drag the selection area** to include at least one corner of any object you want to include.

3   You can **keep the objects grouped** together so they move as a unit: From the Object menu, choose "Group."
To ungroup the collection, from the Object menu, choose "Ungroup."

TASK 10   Select an object in a group

When objects are grouped, individual items can be difficult to select.

- With the black Selection tool, double-click on the object you want.

- To edit text, click in it with the Type tool, even though it's grouped.

TASK 11   Send back and forward

Throughout InDesign, any object in any sort of frame can be in front of or behind any other object. Simply **select the item**, from the Object menu, choose "Arrange," and then choose the action you want.

Now, keep in mind that every single thing you have placed on the page is on its own private layer (completely different from the Layers panel); it's as if each object is on a separate piece of plastic wrap. In general, it's most efficient to choose "Bring to Front" or "Send to Back." Learn the keyboard shortcuts!

TASK 12   Select an object beneath another object

When objects are layered in front or back of others, they can be difficult to select; sometimes you can't even see them.

- Hold down the Command key (PC: Control key) and single-click on the item you want to grab. Each click takes you down through the layers of plastic wrap.

The Pencil Tool

The **Pencil tool** lets you draw as if you were drawing or writing with a pencil on paper. It creates a **path** full of points that you can alter, apply effects to, set curved type along (see pages 192–195), or insert graphics inside of. This tool is great for when you need a simple shape and don't want to—or know how to—use the Pen tools.

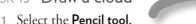

TASK 13 Draw a cloud

1 Select the **Pencil tool.**

2 Press-and-drag to draw squiggly lines all over the page. Try writing your name. You can change the stroke type, weight, and end caps of the line, just as if it were a shape (see page 136).

3 Once you've got the feel of it, draw a cloud shape. Be sure to make the ends meet so you have a closed shape.

4 **To add color to your cloud,** select the cloud with the black Selection tool.

   Open the Swatches panel; select the Stroke box (as explained on page 136). Choose a color for the stroke of your cloud.

   Click the Fill box to select it, and select a color for the inside of your cloud. *Or* select the cloud and place a graphic inside of it, as explained on pages 154.

TASK 14 Smooth out a bumpy line

1 Press (don't click) on the Pencil tool in the Tools panel to get the little fly-out menu; choose the Smooth tool.

2 Press-and-drag over any bumpy parts in your penciled path.

   Or if you know how to use direction handles and points, get the white Direct Selection tool. Drag points and handles to alter the shape.

   Double-click the Pencil tool icon in the Tools panel to get a pane of preferences to experiment with.

I selected these lines drawn with the Pencil tool, then in the Strokes panel, chose the "Cap" called *Round Cap* to make the ends rounded, and the "Join" called *Round Join* to round off the pointy bits.

Pen tools

The Pen tools in InDesign are very similar to the Pen tools in Illustrator and Photoshop, so if you are familiar with those, you can skip this section. If you've never used a Pen tool before, this might be confusing because it operates like nothing you've ever seen. On these two pages I'm going to explain just the *very* bare necessities; please see *The Non-Designer's Illustrator Book* for a much more thorough explanation of the Pen tool as well as exercises for using it.

TASK 15   Experiment with the Pen tools

Create a star shape.

1   Clear your page of other objects. Make sure nothing is selected. Get the Pen tool.

2   In the Swatches panel, choose a black stroke of .5, and a fill of None.

3   Click with the Pen; you get a little dot.

   Click somewhere else, and you see a line between the two clicks. Continue to click until you've created a star shape.

   Make the last click on top of the first one—you'll know you're in the correct position because the Pen tool displays a tiny round circle.

4   To release the Pen from the path, click on any other tool, *or* hold down the Command key and click on an empty space.

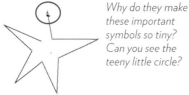

Why do they make these important symbols so tiny? Can you see the teeny little circle?

Once you have a shape, you can alter the points, just as you did on page 139.

5   **Alter the shape:** Get the white Direct Selection tool, then select the star. If you don't see tiny white squares at each point, click again. Press-and-drag to move the points of the star to reshape it.

6   Once you have a shape you want, get the black Selection tool again. You can resize the star, change its stroke and fill, place a graphic inside, and do everything else to it. You can edit its shape forever.

Create a curved shape.

1 Follow Steps 1 and 2 on the opposite page.

2 Do not *click* with the Pen tool—*press-and-drag* a short ways.
This puts down a point *and* drags direction handles out (see below).

3 Continue to press-and-drag points and handles to make a blob.

4 Make the last click/drag directly on top of the first one, but drag
slightly in the opposite direction you've been going (this is to
prevent the line from getting twisted).

5 To release the Pen from the path, click on any other tool,
or hold down the Command key and click on an empty space.

There—a perfect blob.

6 **Alter the shape:** Get the white Direct Selection tool, then select the
blob. If you don't see tiny white squares at each point, click again.

7 This time, use the white Direct Selection tool to click on a point to
display its direction handles. Then drag the end of a direction handle
to alter the shape. Drag the handle outward, inward, or any way.
It takes a while to figure out which way to drag to affect the shape the
way you want. Practice until you kinda know what to expect.

You can also drag the point itself to another position.

Reshape your blob into an amoeba.

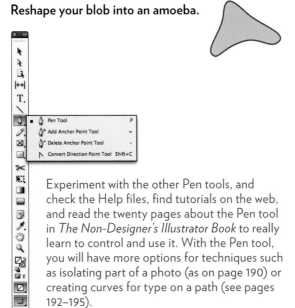

Experiment with the other Pen tools, and
check the Help files, find tutorials on the web,
and read the twenty pages about the Pen tool
in *The Non-Designer's Illustrator Book* to really
learn to control and use it. With the Pen tool,
you will have more options for techniques such
as isolating part of a photo (as on page 190) or
creating curves for type on a path (see pages
192–195).

Graphic Manipulation

Once you place a graphic on a page, you usually need to customize it in some way. You might want to crop it, resize it, rotate it, put it inside a round frame, add a shadow to it, or many other things. For working through the tasks in this section, put several photographs in a folder where you can get to them easily.

Placing images in InDesign

You might think of this action as importing or inserting graphics, as it is often called in other applications. But in InDesign, you **place** a graphic. It's exactly the same process as in other apps, except you get to choose where the image lands on the page. You can even choose to resize it as you place it.

TASK 16 **Place a graphic on the page**

There are several ways to place a graphic on the page, but the steps below explain the primary and safest method (also see page 160).

1 First make sure nothing is selected on the page—single-click on a blank area. You especially don't want an insertion point flashing in the text right now! *Or* to deselect everything, press Command Shift A (PC: Control Shift A).

2 From the File menu, choose "Place…."

3 Navigate to the folder in which you stored your photos. Double-click on the image you want to place.

I scanned an engraving from an old book, then placed it on a photograph of a hand, using Photoshop. I then placed the .tif file on the InDesign page.

4   On the screen, you will see a "loaded" cursor—your pointer is now
    loaded with the graphic image, as shown below.

The cursor even tells you what kind of file it is—vector, raster,
movie, etc! The clue is in the tiny icon in the upper-left of
the thumbnail. In this example, I see it is an Illustrator file.

To put the graphic on the page, single-click anywhere.
*The upper-left corner of the graphic will appear wherever you click
the tip of the pointer to place it.*

5   **Also try this:** Do the steps again to place a graphic. This time, instead
    of clicking to drop the graphic on the page, **press-and-drag with the
    loaded cursor** to place the graphic inside a contained area. You might
    want to do this, for instance, if you have columns on a page and want
    to place the graphic in the exact size you need it. Notice, below, that
    the info box tells you the percentage of the file size as you drag it.

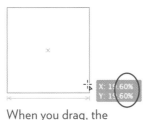

A loaded cursor.

When you drag, the
container stays in the
proportion of the graphic.

The placed image.

6   **Also try this: You can select and place more than one file at a time.**
    The cursor loads up with them all, provides a tiny thumbnail of the
    image about to be placed, and tells you how many files are left.

    If **Smart Guides** are on (see page 11), you can drag to place the first
    item, then as you drag other items, the Smart Guides tell you when
    they are a matching size. Try it!

The cursor tells me there are
three files, and this one is
raster (the paintbrush icon).

7   **Also try this: Place into a shape.** Create or select a shape on the page
    and select it. Go to the File menu to place a graphic, and make sure to
    check the box to "Replace Selected Item." The graphic will be placed
    inside the shape (see page 141). Use the white Direct Selection tool to
    resize (page 149) the brown bounding box of the graphic to fit.

TIP: If the insertion point happens to be inside a text frame, the
graphic will drop into that frame automatically! Just Undo the
action and the cursor will reload with the graphic, ready to re-place.

TASK 17   Now that the image is on the page

1   **To move the photo somewhere,** choose the black Selection tool.

2   Press on the image *anywhere except in the middle;* then drag the graphic around on the page. Drop it in the middle of the page for now.

3   The photo is contained inside a frame, just like all the drawn graphics you worked with earlier in this chapter. This means you can change the frame—**put a stroke on it, color the stroke, reshape the frame,** etc. Try it!

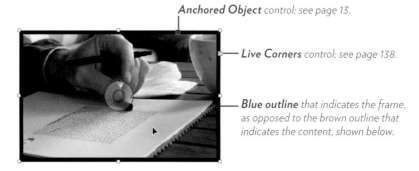

Anchored Object control; see page 13.

Live Corners control; see page 138.

Blue outline that indicates the frame, as opposed to the brown outline that indicates the content, shown below.

Very important: A placed graphic consists of the **content** and the **frame.** Whenever you see a brown *bounding box* (not the frame, but the line that indicates the graphic), that means you have selected the content, not the frame. You can select the content separate from the frame by clicking on the Content Grabber (if it's showing) or by using the white Direct Selection tool. Experiment with this! You can resize the content, move it, rotate it (with the black Selection tool), etc., independently from its frame. Also see page 152.

In general:

Black Selection tool: Select and modify the frame.

White Direct Selection Tool: Select and modify the content.

This is the bounding box of the *content. When you crop an image in InDesign, nothing from the image is ever lost.*

TIP: You can ***turn off the Content Grabber feature*** if you want. Go to the View menu, choose "Extras," and then choose "Hide Content Grabber."

If you accidentally move the graphic out of the frame

If you accidentally press *in the middle of a graphic* to move it, you might find that the graphic moves out of the frame, as shown above.

That's because you dragged on the **Content Grabber** (shown above), that target or donut symbol that appears in the center of the image when your mouse passes over it.

Undo and see if that works. If moving the graphic was the very last thing you did, it will work. If not:

If you can see a bit of the image or the empty frame: With the black Selection tool, click on the bit of image or the frame to select it. You will see the thin, blue bounding box and the handles.

Or if the image has completely disappeared and you can't see the frame: With the black Selection tool, click around on the page where the graphic used to be. When the eight handles of the frame appear, that means it's selected. (*Or* select everything, then pick out that one frame.)

Then go to the Object menu, down to "Fitting," and choose "Fit Content to Frame." The image will snap back where it belongs. It's a good idea to memorize the keyboard shortcut for that command.

If your graphic won't move sideways

If you place a graphic and find that you can't move it sideways, only up or down, that means you accidentally placed the image inside a block of text (which can be a handy thing—check the Help files for *anchored images*—but for now, you need to correct the situation).

If you notice it right away, simply Undo. The image will load itself back into your cursor and you can now click anywhere to drop the graphic on the page.

If you did it a few minutes (or days) ago, get the black Selection tool, single-click on the graphic, cut it, and paste it somewhere else. **Make sure you click in any empty spot on the page** before you paste so the graphic doesn't end up in a text frame again. InDesign maintains the link to the original source file.

Vector graphics resized

A **vector image** created in an application such as Illustrator is built with mathematical formulas instead of with pixels. It has no ppi count (as explained on pages 132–133). You can make a vector graphic as large or as small as you like, and it will always print beautifully.

If you have a vector image in your collection, do this task so you can compare it with a raster image resized, as on the opposite page.

TASK 18 Place and resize a vector graphic

1 Place a vector graphic on the page. You can use an Illustrator file (.ai), a PDF, an EPS file, or any shape or collection of shapes drawn in InDesign.

2 With the black Selection Tool, single-click on the image to select it so its handles show up.

3 Hold down both the Command and Shift keys (PC: Ctrl and Shift keys); press-and-drag a handle. Drag inward to resize smaller; drag outward to resize larger. You can make it as big or as small as you want!

Raster graphics resized

You cannot make a raster image (.psd, .tif, .jpg) much larger than its 100-percent size without it looking pixelated. If you plan to place a lot of photos in your projects, you need to buck up and prepare them appropriately—resize them in Photoshop so they are the correct resolution and close to the size you will use them on the page. I know, it's annoying.

TASK 19 **Place and resize a raster graphic**

1   Place a photograph on the page.

2   With the black Selection tool, single-click on the image to select it.

3   Hold down both the Command and Shift keys (PC: Ctrl and Shift keys); press-and-drag a handle. Drag inward to resize smaller; drag outward to resize larger.

   (The Command/Ctrl key resizes the image, and the Shift key keeps it in the proper proportion.)

4   Check the Links panel (shown on page 160) to see how the **actual ppi** of the image (its resolution at 100 percent) changes to the **effective ppi** (the resolution at which it will print, based on its enlarged or reduced size). For a commercial press, the ppi should ideally be between 250–300 for raster images; your desktop printer is a little less fussy, but a higher ppi will still look better.

   Higher resolution in a raster image is not always better, though! If you have a giant photo that you reduced on the page to an itty bitty thing and the effective ppi is something like 1296, stop it! Make a copy of the photo and reduce it appropriately in Photoshop before placing it.

You can get away with reducing some low-res photos for print. The actual resolution for this image at 100 percent (as shown here) is only 185 ppi.

I reduced this image on the InDesign page and its effective ppi is now 370. This is not the best practice, but can be done in a pinch.

Crop a graphic

Sometimes you want to crop a graphic slightly (or a lot), either for composition or to fit it into a particular space. It's very easy to do.

TASK 20 Crop a graphic

1 Place a graphic on your page.

2 Get the black Selection tool.

3 Single-click on the photo so its eight handles show up.

4 Press on any handle and drag inward to crop the photo in that direction (dragging a corner handle will crop two sides at once). This does not destroy anything—drag the handle back out and the image is still there.

To crop *all sides* of the image proportionally, hold down the Shift key and drag any handle.

To do major cropping, such as to crop a group photo so only one face is showing, you really should do that in Photoshop. If you place the entire large graphic in InDesign and then crop down to the one face, you still have to send the entire large graphic to the printer. This slows down the printing and also makes your InDesign file unnecessarily large.

To show the entire image again, select it. From the Object menu, slide down to "Fitting" and choose "Fit Frame to Content."

Original image. It would look better to remove the backs of the two guys on the right, as well as the distracting bits on the left.

Cropped images.

Expand or compress a graphic

It's rare that you want to expand or compress an image, but it does happen. Sometimes (because the camera adds weight to everyone) you might want to squeeze an image horizontally just a wee bit so a person looks the same size in the photo as they do in person. Or perhaps you want to widen a photograph to fit into the column in your newsletter, but you don't want to crop or resize it.

TASK 21 Adjust a photo's width or height without cropping

1   Place any graphic of your choice.

2   With the black Selection tool, single-click on the photo to select it so its eight handles show up.

3   Hold down the Command key (PC: Control key) and drag any handle. Drag inward, of course, to compress, and drag outward to expand.

To get the correct proportions back, select the image with the black Selection tool. From the Object menu, slide down to "Fitting," then choose "Fit Content Proportionally." This will make the frame a different size from the image, so you need to go back to the Fitting menu and choose "Fit Frame to Content" (check that menu to learn the keyboard shortcut).

Original image.

I compressed this image by more than a quarter of an inch. Now it fits into the allotted space, but doesn't look disproportionate.

Reposition a graphic within its cropped frame

You might want to crop a graphic so the frame fits within your layout, but then you decide you want to see a different portion of that image within the frame. Because InDesign crops images in a *non-destructive* way, none of your picture is ever really gone. Once you have the size frame you want, you can adjust the image inside that frame.

TASK 22 Reposition the graphic in the frame

1   Place a graphic on the page.

2   Get the black Selection tool; single-click on the photo to select it.

3   Drag a corner handle inward so the shape of the photo is smaller. It doesn't matter right now what it looks like.

4   Hover the black Selection tool over the image and you'll see the Content Grabber; it looks like a donut in the middle of the image. **If you have previously hidden the Content Grabber,** no problem—use the *white* Direct Selection tool.

5   Press on the image and hold for a second until you see the shadow of the full image, then drag the pointer and the image will move inside the frame. At any time, you can reposition it again.

Step 3.   Step 4.   Step 5.

This is an alternative crop and rotation that leaves room in the photo to add text. The brown line is the bounding box of the photograph.

Working with a graphic in a frame

Here is an example that uses a variety of techniques to edit and crop an image within InDesign, including the technique on the opposite page.

Original image. To emphasize the compositional similarity between Samuel Clemens Twain and his friend, we need to get rid of the distractions on both sides of the bench. So let's crop it (with the black Selection tool).

Cropped image. The piece of sculpture in the top left and the unknown leg in the bottom right are now cropped out. Using the black Selection tool, I clicked on the Content Grabber donut to get the entire image*, then rotated the image to straighten out the bench.

Cleaned-up image. I right-clicked on the photo to open it in Photoshop (see page 161), where I cloned out the distracting bit of window by Mr. Clemens' shoulder, as well as the lighting fixture above and behind the bench on the right.

Consistent format. To match the rest of the newsletter, I added a 3-point border aligned to the inside (page 136). I used the Eyedropper tool (page 176) to pick up a stroke color from Mr. Clemens, and used the Live Corners control (page 139) to alter the shape of the corner.

*If the **Content Grabber** is not showing, use the *white* Direct Selection tool to select the entire photo, then switch to the black Selection tool to rotate.

Paste Into and adjust

The "Paste Into" command in the Edit menu is very useful. It allows you to paste an element inside a frame, even though the content is a completely different shape from the frame. With the white Direct Selection tool, you can move or resize the inside image easily, within the frame.

TASK 23 Paste a graphic into a frame and adjust the graphic

1 With either a frame tool or a shape tool, create a shape.

   Fill it with None, and a 1-point black stroke. (You can use any fill or stroke you want, actually, but it's easier if you can see the stroke at first; you can always change the stroke and fill later.)

2 Make sure the frame is *not* selected.

3 Place a graphic on the page: Don't click to place it—drag a shape so it's about twice the size of the frame (because many graphics drop onto the page in their full, huge size).

4 Resize the graphic to about the size you want it to be in the final piece.

   Choose a section of the image that you want to appear in the frame you created, and position that section over the top of the frame.

5 Select and cut the graphic.

6 Select the frame. From the Edit menu, choose "Paste Into."

   It pastes into exactly the spot from where you had cut it. Use the white Direction Selection tool to reposition the graphic, resize it, rotate it, etc. Fill the frame with color, if you like.

   If your graphic is not isolated, as this pen is, you won't see any fill in the frame. See page 157 for an example of pasting an opaque image.

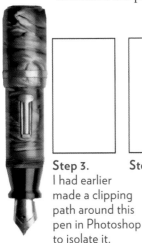

Step 3.
I had earlier made a clipping path around this pen in Photoshop to isolate it.

Step 4.

Step 6.

I filled the shape with color, then added text.

Orlando de Boys.
poet@ArdenForest.com

Transform panel

Everything in the Transform panel is also in the Control panel when an *object* is selected. The options you'll find yourself using most often are the width and height fields for checking and for specifying sizes of objects, and the scaling fields for resizing. The most important thing to recognize in the Transform panel (as well as in the Control panel) is that the measurements must have a **reference point**. InDesign chooses one for you, but you can change it: In the little *Reference Point* icon (also called the **Proxy**), shown below, click on the dot that represents the handle on the object that you wish to stay *stationary*.

TASK 24 Resize and rotate a drawn line (or any frame)

1 Using the Line tool, choose a colored 2-point stroke, and draw a 6-inch line. Watch the width field in the Transform panel to see when your line is 6-inches long (or 36 picas). If you get close, let go, and enter 6i or 36p in the width field; the line (which is still selected) snaps to that exact measurement.

2 Now **rotate** the line: With the black Selection tool, select the line.

In the Proxy, you see three dots selected; click on one of them. That is the reference point *that will stay stationary* when the line rotates.

From the panel menu (or the Control panel), choose "Rotate 90° cw." Did it do what you expect? Undo that rotation, choose another proxy point, and rotate the line again. Practice with this until you can predict what will happen.

3 Place a graphic on the page and use *Scaling* fields in the Transform panel to resize it. Don't forget to pick a proxy, and make sure the chain icon is locked so the scaling is proportional.

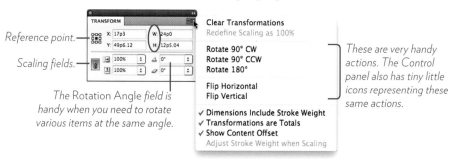

Reference point.

Scaling fields.

The Rotation Angle field is handy when you need to rotate various items at the same angle.

Clear Transformations
Redefine Scaling as 100%

Rotate 90° CW
Rotate 90° CCW
Rotate 180°

Flip Horizontal
Flip Vertical

✓ Dimensions Include Stroke Weight
✓ Transformations are Totals
✓ Show Content Offset
Adjust Stroke Weight when Scaling

These are very handy actions. The Control panel also has tiny little icons representing these same actions.

TIP: When you resize using a measurement in the Transform panel, the content and frame resize, but the blue bounding box around the original graphic doesn't change. **To match the bounding box to the content,** go to the Object menu, down to "Fitting," and choose "Fit Frame to Content." Memorize the keyboard shortcut for this because you'll use it constantly.

155

Align panel

The Align panel is enormously useful. Use it to align objects along their edges or centers, or to distribute the space between objects evenly.

TASK 25 Align a variety of graphic images (or text frames)

1 Draw or place five or six objects on the page.
Get the Align panel from the Window menu.

2 Select all the objects and click the "Align top edges" button
(or align the bottom edges, whichever you prefer), as shown below.

3 Now position the first and last photos at the outer boundaries
of where you want them to fit, as shown below. Arrange them
horizontally for this exercise.

4 Click the "Distribute Spacing" *horizontal space* button (see below).
The spaces between the elements will adjust themselves,
and the first and last photos *will stay in their positions*.

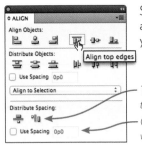

Spend a few minutes checking
all the tool tips so you know what
your options are.

This is the horizontal space button that distributes
the space evenly between selected objects.

Check this button and enter an amount if you
want a specific amount of space between objects.

The photos are placed randomly on the page.

With two clicks, the top edges are aligned and the space
is distributed evenly between the images.

Effects panel

You can experiment endlessly with the effects. The combinations of effects from the dialog box (shown on the following pages) and the ones in the Effects panel (below) are mind-boggling. You can do lots of crazy things, but you can also do very practical things. Below are two tasks using the Effects panel.

TASK 26 Make an object semi-transparent

1 Select an object or objects of any sort.

2 From the Window menu, open the Effects panel.

3 Drag the Opacity slider, or enter a number in the field.

Blending Mode menu.

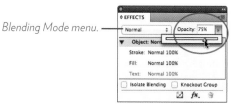

You can also use the Opacity slider in the Control panel.

The lower the opacity, the more transparent the object will be.

TASK 27 Blend an item into the background

This effect doesn't work for all combinations of objects and colors, but can be a lifesaver when it is appropriate. Here's an example:

Let's say you want to use this photo of a cabinet door, below, as the background for a poster, and this scan of a watercolor blot on top of it. But the blot makes a big opaque shape.

Select the blot, go to the Effects panel (above), and choose "Multiply" from the Blending Mode menu. Now you can create the poster.

I cropped the blot, as explained on page 150.

Effects dialog box

You can open the Effects dialog box by choosing one of the effects from the panel menu in the Effects panel (see the previous page), from the Object menu, from the contextual menu when you right-click on an object, and from the small *fx* icon in the Control panel. To experiment, let's apply a drop shadow.

TASK 28 Create a drop shadow on an object

The quickest way to add a drop shadow is to select the object, then click the drop shadow button in the Control bar. It applies the current settings that are in the Effects dialog box, as shown below. But to have more control:

1 With the black Selection tool, select an object.

2 From the Object menu, choose "Effects," then "Drop Shadow...."

3 Make sure the blue bar is highlighting "Drop Shadow." Choose your settings. "Multiply" is the best mode, and an opacity of something like 40% is not too obnoxious. The x and y offsets determine how far the shadow is from the object. Experiment!

Choose to apply the effect to the stroke, fill, text, or the entire object.

*Make sure, after you **check** an item, that you also click its **name** to select the blue highlight bar. Otherwise you won't see the options for that effect.*

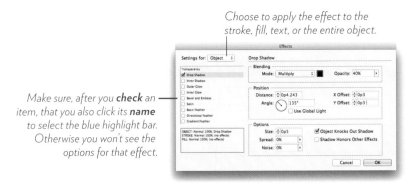

Try some other effects on selected objects, such as the various feathering effects and embossing. Also see page 186 for drop shadow effects on type.

*This is just to show how different combinations of effects and colors can create infinite possibilities. The three variant ovals (that use **Inner Glow**, **Bevel & Emboss**, and **Satin** with a **Drop Shadow**) have a text frame on top that uses "Color Dodge" from the Effects panel, not the Effects dialog box.*

This is a cell phone portrait of my daughter Scarlett (that John Tollett enlarged to two feet tall). Using a smaller version, I did the "Paste Into" technique into an oval frame (see page 154), and then applied the **Basic Feather** effect.

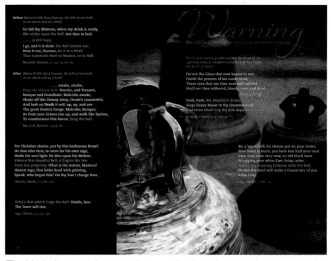

The black shape on this spread was too harsh and it was inconsistent with the rest of the booklet, but without it, the text on the image was difficult to read.

I selected the black shape and gave it a **Gradient Effect** from the right edge. Now the type is readable and the shape is not obnoxious.

Linked images and the Links panel

One very important thing to remember: Even though, yes, it *is* possible to do it, **do not ever copy and paste a graphic** from another application into an InDesign document. Why? Because InDesign doesn't embed images into its files—it merely displays an image as a placeholder with a **link** that tells InDesign where to go to find the actual image. The display on the page and in print comes from the linked image; if there is no link, the image will display crummy, and print even crummier. So never, ever.* Got that?

You *can,* however, drag files from another InDesign file, from Bridge, and even from your Desktop, and InDesign will link to them appropriately. Or you can place a graphic in InDesign, then cut it and paste it (as on page 154) and it will come back in with its link intact.

The Links panel keeps track of every image you place in InDesign. If an image gets updated outside of InDesign (that is, you didn't use the technique on the opposite page), you'll see a yellow warning symbol, shown below. If you change a file's name or move its location, you'll see a red question mark. InDesign prints from the original file, not from the placeholder you see on the page, so the symbols warn you of a discrepancy or a broken link.

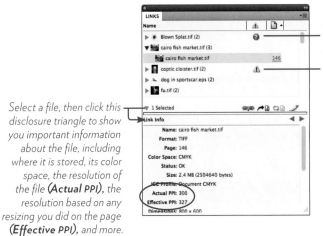

*Select a file, then click this disclosure triangle to show you important information about the file, including where it is stored, its color space, the resolution of the file (**Actual PPI**), the resolution based on any resizing you did on the page (**Effective PPI**), and more.*

*To relink a file to a new graphic because you moved it or changed its name, **double-click the warning symbol** or use the panel menu.*

*If you know that the editing changes to the file are okay, just **double-click the warning symbol** and the file on the InDesign page is immediately updated.*

*Click a **page number** to go right to that page with that graphic selected.*

* OK, the **one exception to this rule** is a vector image created in Illustrator. Turn on the AICB setting in Illustrator's Preferences (under "File Handling & Clipboard"), then when you copy and paste a file from Illustrator into InDesign, the paths are editable in InDesign! If this makes no sense to you, ignore it.

Adjust images in the original application

This is really great. It's for those times when you are looking over the photos in your project and say to yourself, "Omigoodness, my teeth need whitening!" This technique lets you pop into Photoshop, whiten your teeth, go right back to the InDesign page, and la, there you are, teeth whitened. InDesign makes it easy to edit almost any file on the page and updates the link immediately.

TASK 29 Edit an image

1 Right-click on an image that needs an adjustment.

2 In the contextual menu that appears, choose "Edit Original" if the file is internally linked to the original application.

Or go down to "Edit With" and choose an application in which to open and edit the file.

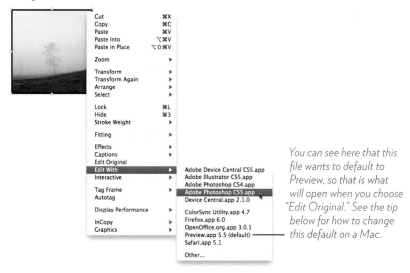

You can see here that this file wants to default to Preview, so that is what will open when you choose "Edit Original." See the tip below for how to change this default on a Mac.

3 Edit your file and save it. If you look at the InDesign page, you'll see that as soon as you save it, the changes are reflected on the InDesign page. When you're happy with the image, save it and close it and go back to InDesign.

TIP for Macs: If your files constantly want to open in Preview, go to your Desktop and click on any .tif file; press Command I to get the Get Info window. Click the "Open with" button. Choose "Adobe Photoshop," and then click the "Change All..." button. All .tif files will now default to your version of Photoshop.

161

Try this!

Below is a page from *Mothering Magazine,* designed by Laura Egley Taylor, that uses many of the techniques explained in this chapter. There is nothing on the page that you don't know how to do! Recreate something like this, using your own images (or ones from CreativeCommons.org) and shapes and text (also see pages 198–199 for a similar example with objects selected).

You could build a cute little shape like this right in InDesign.

Use the Line tool and choose a heavy, wavy stroke.

The dotted yellow oval is a shape with a fill of None and a dotted stroke.

Overlap objects and send them behind and in front of others.

Designed by Laura Egley Taylor for *Mothering Magazine.* Used with permission.

To isolate your image from the background, see page 190.

8 Wonderful Color

Such a world of wonder we live in today, where color can be printed so inexpensively and easily! I won't bore you with stories of how tremendously expensive it was to print color just a few short years ago, and how tremendously tedious it was to design and produce the paste-up to go to press. Suffice it to say that just stopping by a site like PrintPlace.com makes me itch to create something! A thousand rack cards printed in full color on both sides for $75, and all I do is upload the file? Unbelievable! And I can create hundreds of full-color handouts for my workshops right here on my color laser printer? I'm in heaven!

InDesign makes the process of designing in color so satisfying. I hope you enjoy this as much as I do.

*p.s. This chapter tells you how to create and apply colors. If you want to know more about **designing** with color, please see The Non-Designer's Design Book.*

It's important to know the difference between RGB and CMYK colors, as well as process colors and spot colors, so don't skip this short section!

CMYK color

The color model CMYK is what is used for all printed matter (except that from your little inkjet printer). If you have a magnifying glass, look at a magazine cover and you will see tiny rosettes where varying dots of four colors—cyan, magenta, yellow, and black (CMYK)—overlap each other to visually represent the color. It's quite amazing.

These are representations of the four printing plates (cyan, magenta, yellow, and black) that create the photo on the left.

Use CMYK for projects that will be printed on a commercial press, at an online print shop, or on product you might create to sell on sites like CafePress.com or Zazzle.com.

Inexpensive inkjet printers usually prefer RGB (red, green, blue). If you send CMYK graphics to it, they will print up just fine, although the colors might not be exactly what you expect. If you own an expensive color *laser* printer (as opposed to a color *inkjet* printer), CMYK gives you better color; the printer will translate any RGB colors that happen to be in the file to CMYK.

CMYK is based on the color model we see in the world. A red apple appears red because when the light from the sun shines on it, all colors in the spectrum are absorbed *except* red, so red is what gets *reflected* to our eyes.

Color mixing in CMYK works like one would expect: When you mix blue and yellow, you get green.

RGB color

The color model RGB is what is used on all monitors—television screens, computer screens, mobile devices, projection monitors, etc. The color is made of red, green, and blue light coming from inside the device and going *straight into* your eyes (as opposed to CMYK which is light *reflected* off an object).

Use RGB color for graphics that will be displayed on a screen, such as a web site or a PowerPoint or Keynote presentation, a mobile device or an iPad or a television. If the light comes from *behind* the color, use RGB.

You can also use RGB for jobs that you will output on your own inexpensive inkjet printer (although if it uses four toner cartridges, use CMYK).

Color mixing in RGB is crazy: When you mix red and green, you get yellow!

Process color versus spot color

The Swatches panel gives you the option to create Spot Color or Process Color.

A process color is one that will go through the separation process to get printed on the page; that is, it is CMYK that will be divided up into the four dots of the rosette I mentioned on the opposite page.

Spot color is ink from a can on a printing press. In years past when four-color printing (CMYK) was horrendously expensive, we used spot colors at the local print shop to get two-color jobs (say, black and red inks on white paper). With spot colors you can get colors on paper that CMYK can't create very well, such as a deep red, or you can use a spot color as a varnish. This entails a lot more expense, though, because the printer has to use the spot color as a fifth color.

Today, you will rarely run into a reason to have a spot color unless you are creating very expensive and professional work, in which case you're probably not reading this book.

The bottom line is this: Unless you have a specific reason and understand totally why you need a spot color, don't use one. Your inexpensive inkjet printer doesn't really care whether you use RGB, CMYK, or spot colors, but if you're printing to an online print shop or your local professional press, don't use spot colors unless you have a good reason.

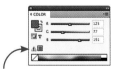

*This tiny yellow symbol is an **out-of-gamut** warning that the color you created cannot be accurately reproduced in that color model. Click the small color box next to the symbol to automatically get the closest color that is in gamut.*

NOTE: **The color you see on your computer screen is not necessarily what will print!** Think about it: What you see on the screen is created with RGB, even if you've specified it as CMYK. What shows up on the paper uses completely different physics.

The color will probably be close, but if you need exact color, you need to learn to calibrate your monitor and work with the commercial press.

A really important thing to remember!

Keep in mind that every object, frame, and text character can have both a Fill color and a Stroke color.

The color gets applied according to 1) what is selected on the page, *and* 2) whether the Container formatting or the Text formatting box is selected, *and* 3) whether the tiny Fill box or Stroke box is selected.

You'll probably forget often to check all three things. Well, maybe *you* won't forget, but I've been working with a page layout application for more than twenty years now and have selected colors at least five billion times, and I still forget to check each box before I apply color. Aaarrghh.

Here are the several places where you can choose whether to apply the color to a **Container** or to **Text** and whether you want it to apply to the **Fill** or the **Stroke** (border). Use the tool that feels more convenient for you.

The color options at the bottom of the Tools panel.

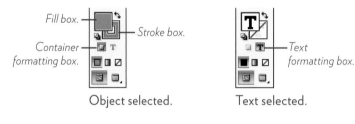

Fill box.

Container formatting box.

Stroke box.

Text formatting box.

Object selected.

Text selected.

The Control panel.

Object selected.

Text selected.

Fill box.

Stroke box.

Click on the arrow to display the Swatches panel.

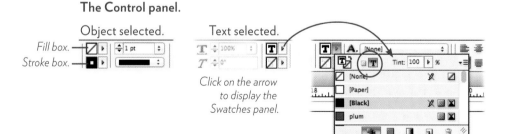

The Swatches panel.

The Color panel.

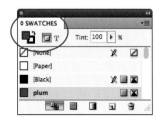

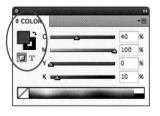

Color panel

There are a number of ways to create and apply colors in InDesign. First, let's walk through the process of using the Color panel.

TASK 1 Open the Color panel

1   Find the Color panel either on your screen, or choose it from the Window menu.

2   If all you see is a color bar, as shown below, click the panel menu and choose "Show Options."

3   If you don't see the CMYK colors, as shown below, click the panel menu again and choose "CMYK."

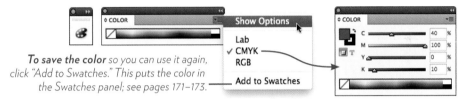

To save the color so you can use it again, click "Add to Swatches." This puts the color in the Swatches panel; see pages 171–173.

TASK 2 Change the color in the Color panel

1   Open the Color panel as explained above.

2   Click the Fill box to bring it forward.

3   Try each of these methods to change the color in the Fill box:

• Drag the sliders for the four colors back and forth to see how the colors get mixed. Try to predict how the color will change as you add or delete more of each color.

• Click in the color bar across the bottom.

• Double-click the Fill box to open the Color Picker. If you've used the Color Picker in Photoshop, you'll see that it's just the same (see page 170 for more about the Color Picker).

4   Click the Stroke box to bring it forward, and change the colors as above.

TASK 3   Apply color to an object

1   The colors in the Fill and Stroke boxes will be applied to the next object you create, so get the Rectangle tool or Ellipse tool and draw a shape (with the tool, press-and-drag diagonally).

2   While that object is *selected,* choose the Fill box and change the color, then select the Stroke box, choose a size for the stroke, and color it.

TASK 4   Apply color to text

There are two ways to apply color to text:

- **To change selected text characters:** With the Type tool, select the characters. Select the Fill box in the Color panel or the Swatches panel. Select the color. (If you want to add an **outline** to each selected text character, choose the Stroke box, choose a stroke weight, and choose a color.)

- **To change all the text in a frame:** With the black Selection tool, select the text frame. Click the tiny **T** (the Text Formatting box) in the Color or the Swatches panel, choose the Fill box, then choose a color. (This only works if the entire story is in one frame; see pages 24–26 about stories in relation to text frames.)

Try both methods several times until you feel confident in the task.

Essentially, the process of applying a color is like everything else in InDesign: **Select the item appropriately, then choose the color.**

I added a half-point purple stroke to these characters in the Zanzibar font, as explained above.

I selected the photo to apply the 4-point stroke and color it black.

I added the bar along the side using the Rectangle tool and applied the black color.

I set the type, turned it ccw (counter-clockwise, using the Transform panel; see page 155), set it in position and adjusted it, and then used the Eyedropper tool to pick up a color in the sky and apply it to the text (see pages 176–179).

Try this!

Recreate objects and text similar to the examples below. Remember, objects will be drawn with whatever colors and strokes are in the Color panel when you start to draw (you can control these defaults, as explained on page 12).

Get in the habit of checking all three things before you change the color: the selected object or text, the Container or Text Formatting boxes, and the Fill and Stroke boxes, as explained on page 166.

This photo advertising "ho-made pies" has a simple 5-point black stroke around it.

I used the "Straight Hash" stroke from the Stroke panel, and clicked the "Align Stroke" button called *Align Stroke to Inside*. The red dot is a separate object, aligned using Smart Guides (page 11).

Brianna Nora

The dingbat beneath the name is a tint of the rose color in the letters (see page 175 on tints).

I placed a graphic with a transparent background (the mermaid) inside a *frame*.

I applied a 1-point black *stroke* to the frame.

I applied a *gradient fill* to the inside of the frame (see pages 180–181).

This uses the "Thin–Thin" stroke with a color in the gap (see page 136). The flower ornament is a 50 percent tint of the text (see page 175). There are three separate objects in this—the oval, the text, and the ornament (which is from the font DB Fancy Flourishes).

I drew this with the Polygon tool, set with 8 sides and 40 percent inset (as explained on page 134). The stroke is a 6-point "Thick–Thin" line, black, and in the Stroke panel I chose yellow for the gap color.

169

Color Picker

You might have used the Color Picker in Photoshop or Illustrator. The one in InDesign is very similar.

TASK 5   Create a color in the Color Picker

1   Double-click on the Fill or Stroke boxes in the Color panel, the Tools panel, or the Control panel. This opens the Color Picker.

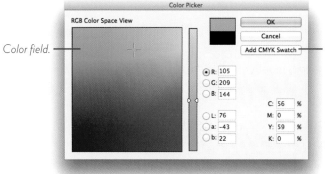

Color field.

This button changes, depending on which value field you click in. For instance, click in one of the CMYK fields to make this button display "Add CMYK Swatch."

These numbers are the **values**, or percentages, of each ink in a CMYK color.

2   Drag around inside the color field; you'll see crosshairs that indicate the color, and that color appears in the top half of the color box.

3   To change the color field, click inside the tall color spectrum bar or drag the sliders up and down.

4   If you know the CMYK or RGB **values** of another color that you want to match (in another file, for instance, or in Photoshop or Illustrator or on a web page), enter the values in the fields shown here.

5   **To save the color as a swatch** in the Swatches panel, click in one of the value fields for CMYK, then click the button "Add CMYK Swatch."

To apply this color to whatever you had selected, click OK.

To make sure a color does not get accidentally applied to something that was selected, click "Cancel."

The Color panel versus the Swatches panel

The Color panel creates local, unnamed colors. This is hugely important. When you create a local, unnamed color and apply it to an object or text, the color exists only in that object. If you want to edit that color, you have to select that object.

Colors in the Swatches panel are global, and all colors are named. When you create a swatch and apply that swatch to an object here, some text there, a style sheet definition, etc., that color is linked back to its swatch. *If you change the swatch, everything that has that color applied will change!* This is a terrific thing, as long as you understand what will happen.

You can customize a swatch color in an individual object: Apply a swatch color to an object, then select that swatch color *in the object or text* and use the **Color panel** to adjust the color. The color in the object or text is no longer a swatch color and will not change if you edit the original swatch. This is very useful for times when you have a main color throughout a piece, but here and there you need that color a little darker or lighter, as in the red example on page 182.

The Swatches panel

Most of the time you will be creating and selecting colors in the Swatches panel because if you are creating a job to be printed, you need to be aware of the color mode and whether a swatch is a spot color or process color (as explained on pages 164–165). This is the Swatches panel; see Task 4 for applying color.

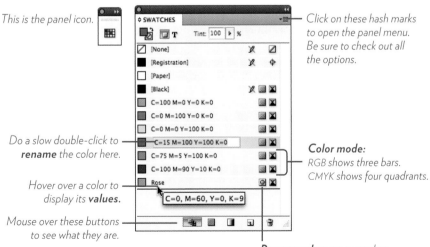

This is the panel icon.

Click on these hash marks to open the panel menu. Be sure to check out all the options.

Do a slow double-click to **rename** the color here.

Color mode:
RGB shows three bars.
CMYK shows four quadrants.

Hover over a color to display its **values**.

Mouse over these buttons to see what they are.

Process colors are a gray box.
Spot colors are a round dot.

171

TASK 6 Create a new color in the Swatches panel

1 Open the Swatches panel, of course.

2 From the panel menu, choose "New Color Swatch."

New Color Swatch

Swatch Name: C=80 M=50 Y=15 K=30
☑ Name with Color Value
Color Type: Process
Color Mode: CMYK

Cyan   80 %
Magenta 50 %
Yellow 15 %
Black   30 %

OK
Cancel
Add

*Change the **type** of color (process or spot) and change the **mode** (CMYK or RGB) in this dialog box.*

*These are the **values** of each of the four inks in a CMYK color. In any other dialog box or in any other application, you can enter these values to create an exact printed match (they will probably look slightly different on every monitor).*

3 Uncheck the box, "Name with Color Value," then change the **name** of the color (you don't *have* to change its name, however).

4 Drag the **sliders** to create your color.

If you know the **values** of the color you want (perhaps you want to match a color from somewhere else), enter those values.

If you're working with a professional press and they have a **color matching system** they want you to use, click on "Color Mode" and choose from thousands of swatch colors in the appropriate list.

5 If you need to, you can change the **Color Type** (process or spot; see page 165) or **Color Mode** (CMYK or RGB; see pages 164–165).

6 If you want to make more than one color, click "Add." The color gets added to the Swatches panel and you can now create another.

When you are finished creating colors, click OK.

You can create hundreds of colors. Give them *identifiable names* so you know what you used them for.

To rearrange the order, just drag the color boxes up or down. If you have a series of colors that belong to a particular project in the job, group them together so you can find them easily.

SWATCHES
Tint: 100 %
[None]
[Paper]
[Black]
rich black
plum
rose pink
section color 1
section color 2
dark plum brown
red dark
lime green

*You can click this button **to create a new color.** The new color is based on the color that was selected when you clicked the button, and it immediately appears in the panel at the bottom of the list.*

Double-click its color box to edit the color.

TASK 7 Edit an existing color in the Swatches panel

There are two ways to **rename a swatch:**

- Double-click on the color swatch to open the "Swatch Options" dialog box. If there is a checkmark in the box labeled "Name with Color Value," uncheck that box, then type in your name. Click OK.

- *Or* click once on the name in the Swatches panel. Wait just a second, then click again on the name. The field opens and you can enter the name you want.

To change its color, type, and mode: Double-click on the swatch color box to open the "Swatch Options" dialog box.

TASK 8 Add Color panel colors to the Swatches panel

If you have created colors in the Color panel and applied them to text or objects, you can easily add those colors to the Swatches panel so you can use them globally: Click the hash mark in the Swatches panel to open the panel menu, and choose "Add Unnamed Colors." They all appear at the bottom of the panel, named with their color values; you can rename them.

Whenever you create a color in the Colors panel, you can use its panel menu to "Add to Swatches," which adds just that color.

Tools panel, double column and single column.

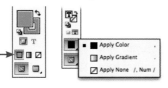

TIP: Here are some handy shortcuts!
1. Select the text or object.
2. Click the Fill box or Stroke box.
3. In the Tools panel, choose one of the following:
   To apply the last selected color, click the *Color* button.
   To apply the last selected gradient, click the *Gradient* button.
   To remove the fill or stroke, click the *None* button.

Working with the colors Registration, Black, None, and Paper

There are three colors that show a crossed pencil, which means you cannot edit nor delete these colors, and a fourth color, Paper, that is special.

Registration: Don't ever use the Registration color unless you know why you're doing it. Whatever is colored Registration will appear on every color plate for printing four-color process jobs. If that doesn't make sense to you, ignore Registration.

Black: Black is black. See the opposite page and page 182 for examples of when you might want a rich black, which is more than black.

None: None is not white; it is an *absence* of color. You can see through None because it's not there.

Paper: The default color for Paper is white, although you can change it. White Paper is opaque; you can click on it because it is actually a thing, a color. It covers up other colors, which means *it lets the color of the paper show through in that place.*

Do *not* use Paper when you want to remove color! Always use None to remove color from an object or text.

You can change the color of Paper, although that color will not print! The point of Paper is to simulate the color of paper that you will print your job on. For instance, maybe you're going to print your flyer onto goldenrod paper. The ink or toner is impacted by the goldenrod color, so if you want to know what it will look like when printed, change your Paper color to goldenrod to approximate the finished piece. The Paper color *does not print.* Leave Paper white until you know you need to simulate the printed page.

TIP: You can **drag** a color box from any panel **and drop** it on an object to change its color!

Make a tint of a color

A tint is when you add white to a color to make it appear lighter in value. There are several ways to do this in InDesign—try each of these techniques!

- **To change the color of an object or text** to a tint value, **select it.** Then in the Color panel or the Swatches panel, change the tint value (the number) or drag its slider. Only the *selected* color is changed.

This is the tint value.

You can also click anywhere in this color bar.

- **To create a Tint Swatch of an existing swatch color,** single-click the existing color in the Swatches panel. From the panel menu, choose "New Tint Swatch…." Change the tint value or drag the slider.

  Because it is based on a swatch, if you change the original swatch, the tint will automatically change at the same time, based on the tint value. You cannot rename a tint that is based on an existing swatch.

- **To lighten an existing swatch** (which *changes* the existing swatch), double-click its color box in the Swatches panel. Hold down the Shift key and drag any slider—all the other sliders will move at the same time, creating a lighter version.

  If you want to keep the original, first **make a copy** of the original color (drag it to the *New Swatch* button, which is next to the Trash icon), and lighten the copy.

When to create a rich black

If you plan to send a job to a high-quality press and it includes areas of black, consider creating a **rich black** with the values 20/20/20/100 (see page 172 about values). They look the same on the screen, but you can see the difference on the printed page:

Black   Rich Black

Take advantage of the Eyedropper tool

The Eyedropper tool is great—use it to pick up colors and formatting from somewhere else in your document. For instance, perhaps you placed a photograph in your brochure and you want to pull colors from that photograph into your brochure; maybe you want a background color and a type color. If you pick the colors from the photograph, you can create a unified look.

Now, when you pick up a color in the Eyedropper, it is applied to whatever happens to be selected at the moment. So it is very important to be conscious of what is selected (as usual)!

TASK 9   Pick up a color and add it to the Swatches panel

1   Place a colorful photo of something on your page.

2   Make sure nothing is selected on any page of your document: With the black Selection tool, click on a blank space.

3   Open the Swatches panel.

Click on the Fill box and the Container formatting box, as shown here:

Fill box. ⟶ *Container formatting box.*

4   Get the Eyedropper tool.

5   Position the very tippy tip of the eyedropper over a color in the photo, then click. The Fill box in the Swatches panel changes to that color, and the Eyedropper flips itself horizontally and looks like it's loaded with ink. **If that's the color you want,** go to Step 5.

This is the part of the Eyedropper that picks up the color.   *This is a loaded Eyedropper.*

If that's not the color you want, hold down the Option key (PC: Alt key) and you'll see the Eyedropper flip back to its unloaded position and it is again "empty" of color, ready to pick up another.

You can keep the Option/Alt key held down and keep picking up colors until you get one you like.

6   When you like the color you see in the Fill box, let go of the Option/ Alt key, open the Swatches panel menu and choose, "New Color Swatch." Uncheck "Name with Color Value," type in a name, and click OK.

TASK 10 Change the color of text in a frame

1 Place a colorful photo of something on your page.

2 Create a few words of text in a frame.

3 With the black Selection tool, click on the text frame.

4 In the Color panel (or in the Swatches panel or the Tools panel), click the Text formatting box and the Fill box (which now has a **T** in it), as shown below.

Fill box. → → Text formatting box.

5 With the Eyedropper tool, position the tip over a color in the photo, then click. The text within the frame immediately changes to that color. **To keep that color,** add it to the Swatches panel as explained in Step 6 on the opposite page.

To experiment with other colors, hold down the Option key (PC: Alt key) and click on other hues. As long as you keep the Option/Alt key down, you can keep changing the color. Let go of Option/Alt to click on an item to apply that color.

Visit Knossos!
Visit Knossos!
Visit Knossos!

There are so many shades of blue to choose from in this image!

Notice that the Eyedropper tool adds a text cursor to its icon when you position it over text. This is your visual clue that if you press and drag over text, the text will change to the loaded color. See the example on page 182.

TASK 11 Change the color of selected text

• To change the color of *selected* text (as opposed to all the text in a selected frame), select the text with the Type tool, then follow Steps 4 and 5 above. Because the text is highlighted, though, you won't be able to see the actual color of the type until you deselect it!

TASK 12 Pick up graphic formatting and apply to objects

You can either load the Eyedropper with attributes and *then* click on things to apply those attributes, *or* you can select text or objects first, then use the Eyedropper to pick up attributes from somewhere else which will be immediately applied to the selected object/s.

1 With the Pencil tool, draw two shapes. Apply different fills and strokes to the shapes.

2 Make sure nothing is selected (either click on an empty space, *or* go to the Edit menu and choose "Deselect All").

3 Get the Eyedropper tool.

4 Click on one of the shapes to load the Eyedropper with its attributes.

Now click on the other shape to pour those attributes from the Eyedropper into that shape.

Check the Eyedropper options

Double-click on the Eyedropper tool in the Tools panel to get the "Eyedropper Options" dialog box, as shown below. These are all the things you can pick up with the Eyedropper! Select and deselect as needed for different projects.

If an attribute is not listed in this dialog box, it cannot be copied with the Eyedropper tool. For instance, corner options are not listed.

TIP: **To pick up only the fill or stroke of an object and no other attributes,** first choose either the Fill box or Stroke box in a panel. Then with the Eyedropper tool, Shift-click the object to pick up the attribute, and Shift-click on the object you want to apply it to.

Try this!

To experiment with the Eyedropper tool, follow these steps. Try to predict what will happen before you click! If something different happens from what you expect, take a moment to figure out why.

1 With the shape tools, create three shapes on the page.

You can either set some defaults before you create them (as explained on page 12), or just create some shapes and see what shows up.

2 Create a fourth shape and customize it to your liking: Choose a fill color, a stroke, a stroke weight, a stroke type, and a stroke color. If you chose a stroke with a gap, perhaps color the gap.

3 With the black Selection tool, Shift-click to select all three of the shapes that you made in Step 1.

4 Now get the Eyedropper tool. *While the three shapes are selected,* single-click on the fancy shape you made in Step 2— its settings will be applied to all the shapes *that were selected.*

You can also use the Eyedropper tool the other way around, as in the Task on the opposite page:

1 Recreate Steps 1 and 2, above.

2 Get the Eyedropper tool, and click on the fourth, fancy shape; this loads the attributes into the Eyedropper.

3 Click on each of the plain shapes; what is loaded in the Eyedropper pours into the shape (or into text as well, if you drag over text).

> **TIP:** Whatever the Eyedropper picks up become your new defaults! This can be crazy-making. Be alert.

Create and apply a gradient

A gradient blends from one color to another, or from different tints of the same color. The gradation can be radical or very subtle. It's easy to overdo gradients because they are so pretty and so fun to create, so try to restrain yourself from littering them all over the place!

You can apply a gradient to text.

Now is the Winter of our Discontent,
Made glorious Summer by this Son of York:
And all the clouds that lour'd upon our house
In the deep bosom of the Ocean buried.
Now are our brows bound with Victorious Wreaths,
Our bruisèd arms hung up for Monuments;
Our stern Alarums chang'd to merry Meetings;
Our dreadful Marches, to delightful Measures.

You can apply a gradient to a text frame.

You can, of course, apply gradients to objects.

The gradient can be *linear,* as in the examples above, or *radial,* as shown to the left, where the color concentrates in a central point and radiates out from there. The central point does not need to be in the center of the object.

TASK 13 Create a gradient

1 Make sure nothing is selected (either click on an empty space *or* go to the Edit menu and choose "Deselect All").

2 Open the Swatches panel, and from the panel menu, choose "New Gradient Swatch...."

3 Single-click on the first color stop, shown circled below.

This color well shows you the color in the selected stop.

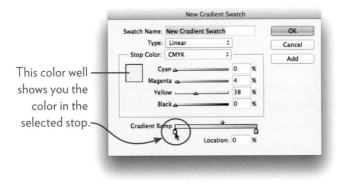

4 Adjust or choose a color: Either drag the sliders, or from the "Stop Color" menu, choose "Swatches" and choose a color from your list.

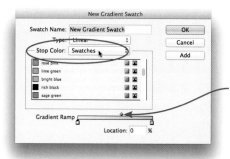

The Gradient Ramp shows you the full range of the gradient.

Drag the **color stops** to change the gradient.

Drag the **midpoint** to change the exact point where both colors are at 50 percent.

5 Click on the end color stop and adjust or choose a color for it.

You can add more color stops: Single-click directly beneath the Gradient Ramp. **To remove stops,** drag them off toward the bottom.

6 Choose whether the gradient "Type" is Linear or Radial, and name the gradient swatch. Click OK.

TASK 14 Apply a gradient

1 As usual, a gradient is applied to whatever has been *selected.* Select text with the Type tool, or use the black Selection tool to select a text frame or an object, or the white Direct Selection tool to select the object inside a frame. Choose the Fill or Stroke box, as usual.

2 Once the item is selected appropriately, choose the gradient swatch you just created. (If you don't see your named gradient in the Swatches panel, click one of the buttons at the bottom of the panel, either *Show Gradient Swatches* or *Show All Swatches.*) The gradient will fill your selection, but don't stop there!

3 Choose the Gradient tool from the Tools panel.

Gradient tool. ── *Gradient Feather tool.*

While the item is still selected, press-and-drag with the Gradient tool over the item. You don't need to start or stop an edge! Experiment with beginning to drag from inside the item or way off to the side, and try dragging way beyond the object. Drag diagonally or from bottom to top. As long as you've got the Gradient tool, you can drag, take a look, drag again, take a look, etc.

4 At any point, you can edit the gradient swatch and all the items that use that color will automatically update themselves.

5 Also experiment with the Gradient Feather tool! Use it just like the Gradient tool—it fades an edge of the gradient. Try it.

Try this!

Below is a simple rack card that doesn't use any features you don't know how to use. It has a rich black border at top and bottom, different colors of type, a small graphic in the .tif format inside an oval with a drop shadow, and some large ornaments tinted just a bit darker than the background color to provide a little texture. The background color is a rectangle the size of the card, sent behind everything else. Can you recreate something similar? A standard rack card is 4 x 9 inches.

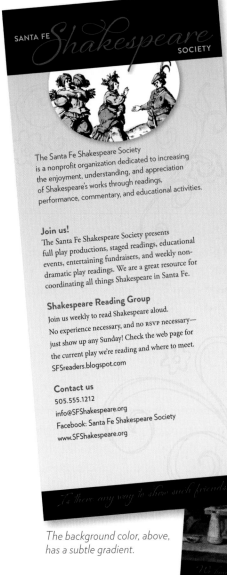

The red color on the rich black is a little brighter than the red I used for the text on the page.

The words "Santa Fe" and "Society" are a 30 percent tint of black.

For the small headings, I picked up the color with the Eyedropper from the image on the flip side.

The title is three different text blocks just because it was easier.

The body copy is one text block that uses spacing, as described in Chapter 3.

The flip side has a large space in which to put labels announcing special events.

The background color, above, has a subtle gradient.

fun and useful
EXTRAS
with **INDESIGN**

InDesign is such a remarkable program. I do hope this book inspires you to go off and learn more about it because there is so much missing from this small introduction! InDesign is one of those applications that makes your computer-time a rich and exciting creative adventure.

You can't wait
for inspiration.
You have to go after it
with a club.

Jack London, novelist, 1876–1916

Creative Tidbits

Really, everything in InDesign is a creative tidbit. But here are a few extra tips for your artistic pleasure. Each page in this chapter is merely an introduction to a particular technique, and I encourage you to spend discovery time exploring the further possibilities.

Also keep an eye out for design projects that use any of these techniques—put them in your Idea File. And keep your wheels turning for ways in which you can push the boundaries of your creativity in InDesign!

Drop shadows and other effects

You learned to apply a drop shadow on graphics in Chapter 7; you can also apply effects to text. Remember, to apply effects to text as an object, you must select the text frame with the black Selection tool. This means the effect will apply to everything in the frame. If you want individual characters within the frame to have a shadow, see the opposite page.

TASK 1   Create a shadow on text in a frame

1   Make a text frame with a headline in it.

2   With the black Selection tool, click on the text frame.

3   From the Object menu, choose "Effects," and then "Drop Shadow…."

4   Make sure the "Preview" button is checked, and start exploring!

You can apply more than one effect to the text.

*Make sure the settings you want to work with are **highlighted in blue!***

*When you check a box, that does not automatically display the settings for that effect. The settings are always shown for the effect with the **blue** highlight.*

The circled settings are the ones you'll probably work with the most, but experiment with all of them!

UNFOLD YOURSELF
Typical shadow: Blending mode is Multiply, 40% opacity, 0p2 offsets, size of 0p5.

UNFOLD YOURSELF
Blending mode is Multiply, 40% opacity, −0p6 and −0p8 offsets, size of 0p2, angle −53.

UNFOLD YOURSELF
Blending mode is Multiply, 40% opacity, dark plum color, 1p5 and 0p10 offsets, size of 0p2, noise of 9%, angle 150.

UNFOLD YOURSELF
Blending mode is Multiply, 90% opacity, dark blue color, 0p0 offsets, size of 0p3, angle 180, text is white.

UNFOLD YOURSELF
This is an Inner Shadow, blending mode is Multiply, 60% opacity, 0p3 offsets, size of 0p4, text is white.

Outline the text for graphic possibilities

As you have surely noticed, there are some effects that you cannot apply to text unless you apply them to the entire frame. But you can turn any character into an **object** and then apply effects just to that object. Follow these steps to apply a drop shadow to one or more characters in a text frame.

THOU ART AN O
WITHOUT A FIGURE

SAID THE FOOL IN KING LEAR

TASK 2 Create a shadow on individual characters

1 Make a text frame with some fairly large text in it, including one or more characters that you want to drop a shadow on.

2 With the Type tool, select the character/s you want to affect.

3 From the Type menu, choose "Create Outlines." That character is now an object.

4 Get the black Selection tool and click on the character. Even if you did this to more than one character, you can only select one at a time.

5 Now you can apply just about any effect: From the Object menu, choose "Effects," and then "Drop Shadow…" (or other effect of your choice). Choose your options and click OK.

TASK 3 Reshape a character outline

When a character is an outline, you can use the white Direct Selection tool to alter its shape. This uses Bezier curves and control points, which I don't have room in this book to explain fully (see pages 142–143), but if you know how to use them from Illustrator or Photoshop, then have at it!

1 Create a large character in a text frame. Create outlines, as above.

2 With the black Selection tool, select the outline, cut it from the text frame, and paste it on the page somewhere (you can alter the points while it's in a frame, but it's tricky).

3 With the white Direct Selection tool, press and drag the anchor points and direction handles.

TIP: **To preserve the original characters as editable text,** you can create the outlines as a copy. Just hold down the Option key (PC: Alt key) when you choose "Create Outlines" from the Type menu. The outlines will appear directly on top of the original.

TASK 4   Type into an outlined text character

The outlines that you created in Tasks 2 and 3 on the previous page can actually be used as text frames.

1 Create a giant character, big enough to put text inside of. Use a bold sans serif or decorative face.

2 With the Type tool, select the character/s you want to affect.

3 From the Type menu, choose "Create Outlines." Now that character is an outline.

4 With the Type tool, click in the outline and type!

> **If nothing happens when you click and type,** you need to change this preference: Go to the InDesign menu, choose "Preferences…," then choose "Type…."
>
> Check in the box, "Type Tool Converts Frames to Text Frames." Click OK.

Now you can click in the outline and type or paste text.

5 Format the text inside the frame as usual.

To change the color of the outlined character, select it with either of the Selection tools (black or white) and choose another color.

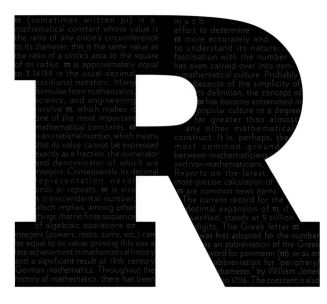

TASK 5   Put a photo inside text characters

Not only can text outlines be used as text frames, they can be used as containers for images. Find a photo on your computer and put it somewhere where you can find it, for use in this task. You're going to create something like one of the examples shown at the bottom of this page.

1   Create a large word in a text frame. Choose a heavy face, very bold. Kern the letters close together.

2   With the black Selection tool, click on the text frame to select it.

3   From the Type menu, choose "Create Outlines." Now every character in the frame is an outline.

4   You can, at this point, place the photo (from the File menu) into the *selected* outlines. But I find it easier to do this:

Do *not* select the text outlines yet. First, get the photo: Go to the File menu and choose "Place…," and double-click your photo.

Click to put the photo on the page, anywhere.

5   Resize the photo to about the size you want it to be when it will be inside the outlines.

6   Position the photo directly on top of the outlines. This is because when you choose the "Paste Into" command, it gets pasted into the exact position it came from, as long as you don't move the outlines.

Once the photo is in position, go to the Edit menu and choose "Cut."

7   With the black Selection tool, select the outlined characters.

8   Go to the Edit menu and choose "Paste Into." Voilà!

9   Get the white Direction Selection tool. Click on the photo to get its *brown* outline. Drag the image into the position you want, or resize it from one of the brown corners.

10   To resize the entire graphic, outlines and all, use the black Selection tool. Don't enlarge it past the appropriate resolution of the graphic, as explained on page 133.

Isolate a photographic image

It enhances your design options if you know how to isolate an element in a photograph. This technique uses the Pen tools, to which there is a much-too-brief introduction on pages 142–143. If you do feel comfortable using the Pen, this is a very useful procedure.

TASK 6 Isolate an area of a photo

1 Place a graphic on the page (File > Place).

2 Get the Pen tool.

3 Choose a 1-point or half-point black stroke and a fill of None.

4 Draw a path around the object you want to isolate, on top of the photo.

5 Select the photo, then cut it (from the Edit menu), leaving the path behind. Don't move the path.

6 With the black Selection tool, select the path.

7 From the Edit menu, choose "Paste Into." Ta da!

When you move the entire object, make sure to use the black Selection tool. To adjust the position of the photo *inside* the path, use the white Direct Selection tool.

You can use the white Direction Selection tool to adjust the paths at any point.

If you don't want to see the path, select it with either the white or black Selection tools and give it a swatch color of None.

This is the original photo. The art is stunning, but the wall detracts from it.

I made the path around the art extra thick here so you can see it.

Finished result. The path is still there (.5 pt. and None) and the entire image is still there, but hidden.

Wrap text around an object

You can wrap text around any sort of object, including drawn objects, imported graphics, and even text frames. The wrap is actually applied to the object, *not* to the text; the object holds a boundary around itself to repel the text. This means if you move the object onto another body of text, that new text will wrap around the object boundary. This is the simplest form of text wrap, just to get you started using it.

TASK 7 Wrap text around an object

1 Create a text frame full of small type, and justify the text.

2 Then place a photo or draw any sort of shape on the page. Position the graphic so it overlaps the text at least halfway.

3 With the black Selection tool, select the object.

4 From the Window menu, choose "Text Wrap."

5 Click the button to *Wrap around object shape.*

6 Explore the options in the "Wrap To" and Contour "Type" pop-up menus.

7 If you know how to use the Pen tools and the white Direction Selection tool, you can create new points and customize the shape.

SHALL BE GONE TOMORROW!

Once upon a time, a young man visiting the kingdom of Patan was very much surprised to see that an old man, named Raghu, was harnessed to an oil-crushing wheel and was made to go round and round like a bullock or buffalo.

"How long can you pull on like this?" asked the visitor. The old man replied, "Don't worry, my young man, all this shall be gone tomorrow!"

Some time later, the young man visited the place again, and this time also, he was in for yet another surprise. He found the same Raghu, who had earlier been working at the oil-mill like an animal, had now become the mill's owner himself! As he congratulated Raghu for his rise in life, the old man replied, "Thank you, young friend, but all this shall also be gone tomorrow".

Next time the young man came back to the same town, he was further amazed. For, Raghu, the old man, had already become the king of Patan! "How come, my old friend? he asked. Raghu replied that the previous king of Patan had died and, according to the local custom, a new king was to be chosen by the royal elephant by garlanding whomsoever the animal chose. When everyone amongst the townsfolk had gathered at the large city-square, the elephant walked straight towards Raghu, threw the garland around his neck and turned back!

"Oh, I am so happy to hear this exciting story, Raghuji. My hearty congratulations!"

But old Raghu embraced the young man and said, as usual, "Never mind, all this shall be gone tomorrow!"

Sometime later, the young man happened to pass by the same town once again. But, to his utter surprise, all he saw there was a heap of rubble and ruined houses. There was no trace of the palace, or the town, including Raghu.

Shocked to the extreme, he made enquiries with the few people he met and learnt that an earthquake had destroyed almost everything in that city-state.

Now the wisdom of Raghu's repeated sayings dawned on the young man, and he said to himself, "Yes, all this shall be gone tomorrow"!

MORAL: Nothing lasts forever.

This is one text frame that I divided into two columns using the "Text Frame Options" shown on page 33.

The text wrap picked up the path I created on this photo, and I expanded the boundary in the Text Wrap panel.

Type on a curve

Type on a curve is not only fun to create, it's useful. You might want to curve type around a logo, a seal, or a patch, add energy to an ad or poster, or simply draw attention in an appropriate way. InDesign makes this easy to do—as long as you follow the directions and are aware of the visual clues in the cursor.

TASK 8 Create a path and set the type

Text gets set along a *path,* which is a vector line of any sort. A path is made whenever you create any frame, shape, or draw a line with the Pen tool or the Pencil tool. (You cannot, however, create type on a *compound path,* which is when several paths are combined into a single object. For instance, when you convert type to outlines, as shown on pages 187–189, the type becomes compound paths.)

So your first step is to create a path. Let's start with an oval.

1   Get the Ellipse tool. Make sure nothing is selected, and then choose a Fill of None, and a Stroke of 1 point in any color. Choose 12-point type.

2   Draw an oval several inches wide, with a gentle arch.

3   Get the Type-on-a-Path tool (it's under the regular Type tool).

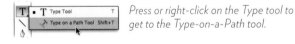

Press or right-click on the Type tool to get to the Type-on-a-Path tool.

4   Position the tool on the line, toward the left, upper edge of the oval; you will see a teeny tiny little **+** sign when you are positioned properly on the line, as shown below-left.

Press-and-drag the tool to the opposite side of the oval. You will see the in and out ports on the text brackets, as you do on a regular text frame, as shown below-right. Let go when the right bracket is positioned where you want the text to end.

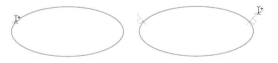

If your default text has an alignment (such as centered) or an indent, the text won't begin at the beginning. Just as you would with straight text, adjust your text settings.

5 As soon as you let go, the text insertion point flashes at the beginning of the line. Start typing. Ta da! For this task, continue typing until the text doesn't fit anymore and you see the red plus sign in the Out Port, as shown below. Uh oh, overset text.

6 Get the black arrow Selection tool, and single-click on the text. Position the tip of the Selection tool on either of the brackets at the ends of the text frame—do *not* position the tip over the in or out port. A *really* tiny symbol appears in the cursor when you are in the correct position, as shown below. Drag the bracket until all the text appears.

Look for this tiny symbol: ⊣ or ⊢ depending on which end you position the pointer.

7 Now that the text is set on the path, **format** it as usual: Select the text and change its color, the font, center it, kern it, etc. You will probably have to adjust the end brackets as you change the formatting.

8 **To get the Options dialog box,** select the text with the black Selection tool, then double-click on the Type-on-a-Path tool in the Tools panel. Experiment with these options! Make several copies of your text (Option- or Alt-drag) and see how the various effects compare.

You can also get this dialog box from the Type menu; choose "Type on a Path, then choose "Options."

The "Spacing" feature applies only to text positioned on a tight curve.

9 Select the oval with the black Selection tool and change its color to None. The oval is still there, but now all you see is the text.

From the Options dialog, above, I chose the alignment called "Descender" to move the text away from the path. The text is centered.

Using the Edit command, "Paste Into" (see page 154), I pasted a photo inside the oval.

I used the Eyedropper (pages 176–177) to pick up a color from the photo and apply it to the text.

TASK 9 Set text all along a circle

In the first Task, you defined the space in which to type. In this short Task, you're going to simply click and start typing.

1   Get the Ellipse tool and draw a circle (hold down the Shift key to make a perfect circle).

2   Fill the circle with None, and give it a 1-point Stroke of any color.

3   Get the Type tool. Choose 10- or 12-point type, depending on the size of your circle (bigger circle, bigger type).

From the Type menu, choose "Tabs" and make sure all the indent markers are all the way to the left.

From the Paragraph specs in the Control panel or the Paragraph panel, choose a left alignment.

You can, of course, do all of the above after you set the type instead of doing it before.

4   Get the Type-on-a-Path tool (it's under the regular Type tool).

5   Position the tool at the top of the circle; you will see a tiny **+** sign when you are positioned properly on the line.

Click. Type. The text goes all the way around the circle. Follow Steps 6–9 on the previous page to format your text and shape.

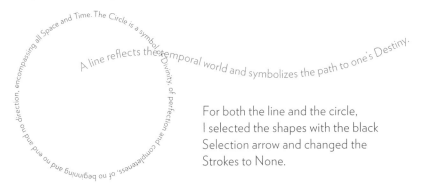

For both the line and the circle, I selected the shapes with the black Selection arrow and changed the Strokes to None.

TASK 10 Set text along a line

1   Using the Pencil tool or the Pen tool (see pages 141–143 for how to use the Pencil and the Pen tools), draw a curved line.

2   With the Text-on-a-Path tool, click on the line, then type!

3   With the white Direct Selection tool, move or adjust the points on the line as explained on pages 139 or 143.

TASK 11 Reposition the text on a curve

You can **reposition the text** on the line at any time. For this Task, use the circle of text you created in Task 9, or recreate another circle of text.

1 With the black Selection tool, single-click on the text so you see all the handles. Find the teeny weeny little tiny blue marker in the middle of the line of text, as shown below-right.

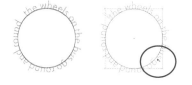

Can you see the itty bitty blue line?
It's at the center point of the text.
When the pointer is positioned over it,
the cursor displays an even tinier marker: ⊥

2 Position the cursor over that tiny blue center bracket (make sure you see the tiny symbol, shown above), then press-and-drag the bracket *outside* the text. This moves the end brackets around the shape or back and forth on a line, as shown below-left. When the end brackets are positioned where you want the text to begin and end, let go.

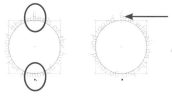

Keep an eye on the end
brackets; let go when they are
positioned where you want.

3 If, during the process above, you drag the cursor toward the *center* of the shape, you'll notice that the text **flips to the inside.** If you want this, great—just let go of the pointer. If not, drag the cursor back to the outside of the text and it will flip back to its original position.

This might be exactly what
you want at some point.

TIP: You can only set one line of type per path, but you can thread the lines just the same as you thread regular text frames (pages 24–28).

Libraries

When you find you use a certain element over and over, you can create a Library to keep it in and make it easy to access. You can store drawn shapes, grouped items, logos, text frames, even ruler guides. Each element preserves all attributes that you gave it, and when you drop it into another document, all those attributes go with it, including any file link information.

If you remove the element from the InDesign document, its thumbnail stays intact in the Library, still available for you to use.

TASK 12 Create a new Library and put things in it

1 From the File menu, choose "New," and then "Library…."

2 Name the library. This name will display in the Library panel tab, so give it a descriptive title that will tell you what is in it.

You can have as many Libraries as you want, perhaps categorized for different projects.

3 With the black Selection tool, select an item on the page to put into the Library. You can either drag-and-drop it into the Library pane, or click the *New Library Item* button.

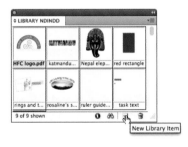

Option-click (PC: Alt key) the *New Library Item* button to get an information pane where you can name the item and add keywords to make it easy to search and find later. (If you forget to do that, you can always double-click an item once it's in the Library to get the information pane).

4 To place an item from the Library onto a page, just drag it out of the Library pane. *Or* select an item in the pane and use the panel menu.

Try this!

If you're in a class, use the features explored in this chapter (and the others), and discover something new! Experiment with all the options, try something wild, combine effects, push things to the limit. For instance, find out more about the text wrap feature and all the things you can do with it; learn to use the Pen tool and create paths for isolating graphics and curving lines of text, discover what else can be done with the Paste Into command or outlined text characters. Share the results with your classmates.

10 Try this!

This chapter is filled with design projects that you can recreate as practice or use as templates for your own work. As in any field of art, recreating a piece teaches you so much about working in that field and with those tools.

This chapter should also inspire you to create your own Idea File—pages you have torn from magazines, printed from the web, received in the mail, copied from a book cover, etc. Whenever you see something that you recognize as good design, file it away for yourself. When you have a project to work on, pull out your file and browse through it for ideas. Don't worry about copying—the project inevitably becomes your own as you develop it with your own information and graphics.

If you've read *The Non-Designer's Design Book,* make notes on these pages where each design uses contrast, alignment, repetition, and proximity.

You know how to do this!

The page below, designed by Laura Egley Taylor and Melyssa Holik for *Mothering Magazine,* has nothing on it that you don't know how to do (if you worked through the tasks in this book, that is!). On the opposite page, everything is selected on the original page so you can see how Laura put it together. With a few images from your own iPhoto collection or CreativeCommons.org, you can create something very similar, but with your own focus on a topic.

There are only two fonts on this page: Myriad and Wiesbaden Swing. Myriad is an OpenType sans serif font with a wide variety of styles, and it contrasts beautifully with the soft and curvy script face.

This is a series of short colored rules lined up and grouped.

A photo was pasted into a round frame; see page 154.

This is the oldstyle version of the numbers.

Two of the frames on this page have dotted strokes.

The text frame for "Listen up!" was filled with Paper color to block out part of the stroke behind it.

Designed by Laura Egley Taylor for *Mothering Magazine.* Used with permission.

You can see there are a number of tints used to lighten objects in the background (see page 175 on tints). The colors in the text and objects were picked up from the photos with the Eyedropper tool, as you learned to do on pages 176–179.

It's always good to have a font that includes (or is entirely made up of) ornaments. Go to **MyFonts.com** and search for "ornaments" to find ornamental fonts such as *DB Fancy Flourishes* or *Creepy Ornaments*, or fonts that include ornaments, such as *Belluccia* or *Lady Rene*.

If you don't have a photo with a transparent background, you can create your own clipping path to remove the background; see page 190.

You can see there are a number of shapes drawn right in InDesign (see Chapter 7).

This image was painted in Photoshop and then placed on the InDesign page.

ON THE WEB : May–June at Mothering.com

With warm summer breezes on our minds, the *Mothering* staff have been busier than ever developing new ways for you to enjoy the *Mothering* content you love. Check out what's in store online for May and June—visit *Mothering.com/links* for direct access to everything mentioned in this section.

Better than ice cream

As the days warm up, you'll appreciate this easy trick for mom-approved frozen treats. Low in sugar and high in coolicious flavor, these yummy desserts will have your kids clamoring for more.

50 ways to keep your kids reading all summer

Remember those seemingly endless childhood days of summer, when you couldn't wait to retreat to the shade of a backyard tree with a glass of lemonade and a favorite book? Well, despite the faster pace of today's world, your children can still enjoy the simpler pleasures of reading. Check out these useful suggestions for helping them do so.

Listen up!

Mothering is making some noise—a new audio version of the magazine is in the works, along with an electrifying new *Mothering* radio show, to be unveiled in June. To listen to our special radio report on Safe Babywearing, click on Radio.

Cloth diaper how-tos

Cloth diapering looms large in this issue of *Mothering*. So, after you've enjoyed "The Diaper Dilemma," by Jennifer Margulis, don't miss our one-of-a-kind how-to video feature, "Diapering Naturally." Also register for our webinar on cloth diapering, scheduled for June 7. And while you're at it, send your diapering questions to our cloth-diapering expert, Eden Haywood-Bird.

blue
TRAVEL TIPS FOR FLYING WITH YOUR CHILDREN

Traveling with your child by plane doesn't have to be a dreaded nightmare. Check out our tips for making those trips manageable, safe, and even fun.

Ask an Intuitive

Fundraising is fun! Support our discussion boards while getting insight from intuitive Jamie. Ask her your most confounding questions at MotheringDotCommunity today.

facebook.com/ mothering magazine

Twitter.com/ MotheringMag

6 | mothering ◆ May–June 2010

To get more petals on this flower, a copy was made, pasted into place, then rotated.

The page number and magazine name/ date is on a master page, as explained on pages 14–15.

199

Flyer

You wouldn't want to create a flyer with a solid sheet of color that bleeds off all edges if you have to print it on your desktop printer—five copies and your toner would be gone! But if you're using an online printer who is going to print in full color, then by all means, use lots of bold color.

Designed by Laura Egley Taylor for *Mothering Magazine.* Used with permission.

For a border around a photo, as in this flyer, use the black Selection tool. Click on the photo, then drag the handles (circled, below) in the centers of the edges outward. Fill the graphic frame with a color.

Dana Gwendolyn

TIP: I realize that new designers might look at a beautifully simple page as the one above and think, "Okay, I see how I could recreate it, but I could never think up the layout!" That's why you need to start an Idea File and make notes about the good and bad design you see. Design works by osmosis, as long as you are consciously noticing.

Text-heavy page

Just because there is a lot of text on a page doesn't mean it has to be boring. Most of what makes lengthy text appear elegant and readable is based on the spacing features you learned in Chapter 3—spacing between the letters, between the lines, between the paragraphs—and between the various graphic elements, as discussed in *The Non-Designer's Design Book.* For your own project, try adding subheads (using style sheets, of course) to guide readers through the text.

This is a drawn line using the stroke type called "Wavy," about 6 points thick.

This photo has a text wrap on it; see page 191.

You know how to format text as shown in this sidebar (tall text frame, flush right, fixed leading).

The giant quotation marks are set in separate text frames and sent behind the main text.

Designed by Laura Egley Taylor for *Mothering Magazine.* Used with permission.

Notice the first paragraph of the text is not indented, which is a typographical standard of excellence. Also notice the text uses a small indent, not the half-inch indent (or five spaces) you might have been trained to do. You can use space between the paragraphs OR an indent—never both!

Table of contents

Magazine tables of contents have got to be one of the most fun projects to design, and one of the most overlooked. There should be prizes for tables of contents. Next time you're in the dentist's office, instead of reading the magazine articles, study the contents pages. Make notes about the design, the typefaces used, how the page numbers are presented, what impression is projected, and is that impression appropriate for the magazine, and why?

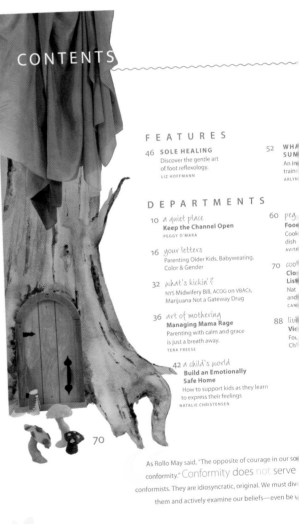

Laura picked up elements from the inside pages to illustrate the contents, as you can see by the following page.

With the style sheets and the "Next Style" feature you learned in Chapter 6, you can type these contents without having to stop to apply a lick of formatting:

Use a Nested Style so the page number appears in the Myriad oldstyle numbers, then switches to the Wiesbaden Swing font automatically for the title.

When you hit a Return, it picks up the next style sheet for the descriptive copy.

When you hit the next Return, it picks up the byline style sheet.

Hit the next Return and it picks up the page number style sheet again and starts all over!

This text frame is a master page element, of course.

CONTENTS

FEATURES

46 **SOLE HEALING**
Discover the gentle art
of foot reflexology.
LIZ HOFFMANN

52 WHA
SUM
An in
train
ARLYN

DEPARTMENTS

10 *a quiet place*
Keep the Channel Open
PEGGY O'MARA

16 *your letters*
Parenting Older Kids, Babywearing,
Color & Gender

32 *what's kickin'?*
NYS Midwifery Bill, ACOG on VBACs,
Marijuana Not a Gateway Drug

36 *art of mothering*
Managing Mama Rage
Parenting with calm and grace
is just a breath away.
TERA FREESE

42 *a child's world*
**Build an Emotionally
Safe Home**
How to support kids as they learn
to express their feelings
NATALIE CHRISTENSEN

60 *peg*
Foo
Cook
dish
AVITA

70 *coo*
Clo
Lis
Nat
and
CAN

88 *livi*
Vic
Fou
Ch

70

As Rollo May said, "The opposite of courage in our so
conformity." Conformity does not serve
conformists. They are idiosyncratic, original. We must div
them and actively examine our beliefs—even be

2   mothering | November–December 2010

Notice how Laura has used decorative elements behind the main elements. The decorative pieces all use tints of colors (see page 175) or the opacity of the object has been lightened (page 157). This lets the decorations add texture and interest to the page, yet not overwhelm the visual impression.

52

42

60

16

keeping it
green

Mothering is a leader in environmentally responsible paper use, and has been creating a demand for it for nearly 20 years. Circulation Director John McMahon works with the Magazine Paper Project at Co-op America and advises other publishers about recycled paper. In recent years, recycled paper has achieved new levels of brightness and opacity that rival those of papers made from virgin fiber. However, only 5 percent of magazines are printed on recycled paper, and only 1 percent on paper made from post-consumer waste (PCW).

Our paper, Leipa Gloss, is manufactured from 95 percent PCW and 5 percent recycled content. The PCW comes from de-inked magazines, newspapers, and commercial and household paper waste. Only a handful of paper plants in the world manufacture PCW.

When made with Leipa paper instead of new trees, every issue of *Mothering* saves:

- **34,000 pounds of virgin fiber**
- **205 trees**
- **18,000 pounds of solid waste**
- **21,000 gallons of water**
- **26,600 kilowatt-hours of electricity**
- **33,800 pounds of greenhouse gases**

Our printer, Quad Graphics, is a leader in environmental stewardship. In 2008, the Wisconsin Environmental Working Group recognized Quad as a Business Friend of the Environment, and *Graphic Arts Monthly* recognized the company as being among the Top 5 Print Industry Brands associated with sustainability.

November–December 2010 | mothering.com   3

This is a text frame with a dotted stroke and a color fill. The tree has an opaque background, but Laura created a clipping path around it (see page 190) to isolate the image.

ON THE COVER

Pennsylvania photographer Kathy Wolfe shot this photo of two-year-old Felicity tenderly cuddling a doll from Blabla. To see more of Kathy's work, go to *www.kathywolfephotography.com*.

mothering
best natural toys

MY
ATION
avel sans
mobiles

ly
delicious
r table.
AN

ke wonder

al

rdice, it is
ey are not
selves for
our mind.

— Peggy O'Ma.a
l Open," page 10

*Designed by Laura Egley Taylor for *Mothering Magazine*. Used with permission.*

Inside spread

This is an inside spread in an issue of *Mothering Magazine*. I included this one because of its beautiful use of a large element and plenty of white space. New designers seem to have trouble making elements **LARGE**, and they also have trouble letting the white space be there. So here is an example to recreate with your own images, text, and topic. Let there be White Space! And Big Stuff!

As Laura demonstrates below, the beauty of the Big Stuff is usually in direct proportion to its contrast with the Small Stuff.

You learned how to put a photo inside text characters in Chapter 9. Here, Laura has placed a different photo into each character.

Designed by Laura Egley Taylor for *Mothering Magazine*. Used with permission.

Advertising

A professional (and affordable) photo from a vendor such as iStockPhoto.com, Shutterstock.com, or Veer.com can make an effective ad easy to create. An image like the one below already has the background removed. You can practice with free images from CreativeCommons.org, and it's possible you can even find exactly what you need there for a real job.

This piece consists of three text frames and a photo.
Having interesting fonts on hand (like Profumo, above)
helps a lot.

Booklet handouts

InDesign has a fabulous feature for creating booklets. If you have a desktop printer that will print double-sided automatically, oh joy! Create a document with a page count that is a multiple of four, in "Letter - Half" size, "Portrait" (tall) orientation, with facing pages. Use master page items and automatic numbering as explained on pages 14–15. Use style sheets (Chapter 6) for the text.

When you're ready to print, go to the File menu and choose "Print Booklet…" to choose your specs (most likely 2-up Saddle Stitch with its default settings). Click "Print Settings…" to make any changes, and then click the "Printer…" button to get to your specific desktop printer settings; check the box for two-sided printing. I love making booklets. :-)

*These are from a 20-page booklet I used
as a discussion point for a presentation.*

Half-sheet flyer

For flyers you plan to print on your desktop printer, consider a half-sheet size. Create the flyer on half of a regular letter-size document, and when finished, select all, then Option-drag (PC: Alt-drag) the entire thing to the other side of the page. Cut them down the middle when printed.

A distinctive font in a large size can make a huge difference when competing with other flyers on a bulletin board. The tall, skinny size makes a visual impact as well. And use color!

This is not a text frame sitting on a rectangle. I filled the text frame itself with color, centered the text horizontally, and used the Text Frame Options to provide space above and below the text (as explained on page 33).

This text is in one frame. This is easy to do when you know how to use the spacing features in InDesign (Chapter 3) and tabs (Chapter 4).

Notice this entire horizontal piece is one text frame. I used a Paragraph Rule (page 219) above the "Life Guidance" line, and Space After (page 55) in the cell phone style sheet. Because I used a style sheet (Chapter 6), I was able to add or delete points of Space After to quickly make it fit.

207

Experiment!

InDesign makes it easy to experiment with lots of possibilities for any job. Take your elements (or the elements your client wants) and keep playing with them—the more you play, the more ideas that appear. Look through your Idea File and get even more ideas. The possibilities are infinite!

11 Going to Press

If you really are a new designer, chances are you're not creating really complex jobs that need to be babied through a million-dollar printing press. On the other hand, with the combination of InDesign in your hands and online print shops that can print your uploaded files in gorgeous full-color, there's no reason for you to limit yourself.

If you follow the guidelines in this chapter, your work should print just fine.

I know I've said it before, but I'll say it again—it is so exciting to be living in a world where we can print in full color for such affordable prices! Go to your room and design something!

Printing to your desktop printer

If you plan to print to your **inexpensive little inkjet**, you really don't need to do anything but set up your printing specs in the Print dialog box, then click the Print button. The paper and quality that you choose in the Print dialog boxes for your specific printer make a huge difference in the output, so be sure to check them (see below).

If you have a more **expensive desktop laser printer**, you have even more control over the quality. Surely you have downloaded the latest print driver so you have options for quality control. In the Print dialog box, click the button at the bottom, "Printer…," to get access to your specific printer options. InDesign will yell at you (a little message pops up), but that's okay.

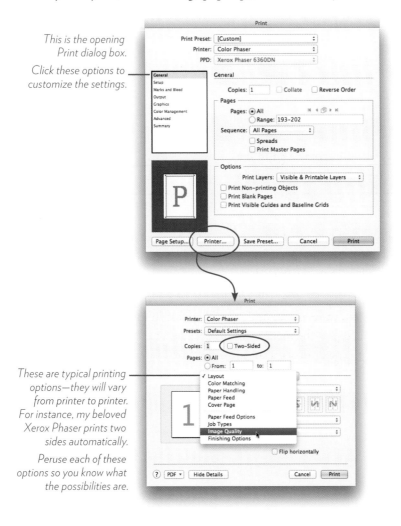

This is the opening Print dialog box.

Click these options to customize the settings.

These are typical printing options—they will vary from printer to printer. For instance, my beloved Xerox Phaser prints two sides automatically.

Peruse each of these options so you know what the possibilities are.

- If you've used an **OpenType font** with a huge character set, be sure to set the Fonts/Download option as "Subset," as shown below.

  If you find that **really large graphic files** choke your printer, change the Images/Send Data option to "Optimized Subsampling."

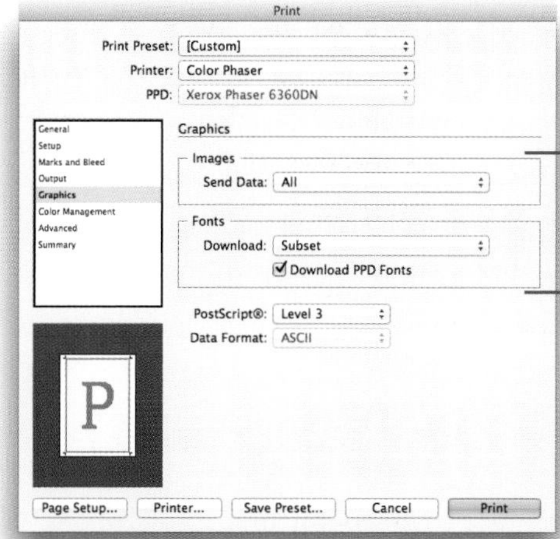

Adjust these specs if large font files or graphic files cause trouble (like very slow printing, or no printing at all).

- **Page Setup:** It's always a good idea to check the Page Setup options before you print a new job for the first time. Click the "Page Setup…" button and make the simple adjustments, if necessary.

- **Print Presets:** If you print a certain type of job regularly, such as horizontal postcards or lengthy reports, set up your specs exactly how you want them, then click the "Save Preset" button at the bottom of the dialog box; name that preset collection of options.

  From then on, those preset options will appear in the "Print Preset" menu at the top of the main Print dialog box, or you can choose it from the File menu to send the job straight to the printer.

Preparing your files for a commercial press

If you plan to print anywhere besides your desktop printer, clean up your files before sending them off. Here is a list of the things I check:

- **Check the Links panel** to ensure that all graphics are linked properly. Also check that you don't have any .jpg or .gif files in the document.

- **Get rid of all unnecessary swatches, character styles, and paragraph styles:** Go to each of the panel menus and choose, "Select All Unused." InDesign will highlight all the unused swatches and styles. While they are selected, Option-click (PC: Alt-click) the Trash icon. In the Paragraph Styles panel, if "Basic Paragraph" is selected, you can't throw anything away, so with the Command key held down, single-click on "Basic Paragraph" to *deselect* it from the collection, and then throw the rest of them away.

- **Make sure all Swatches** are CMYK. If you have an RGB or LAB color, double-click it and change it to CMYK. You can select more than one color to apply this change to them all at once.

- **Make sure all Swatches** are process colors, not spot colors. If you have a spot color, double-click it (or select and double-click several at once) and change it to "Process" (assuming you are printing CMYK).

- **Check the fonts in the document:** Use "Find Font…" from the Type menu to make sure there are no missing fonts and to make sure you haven't used any TrueType fonts unnecessarily.

- If the press you use doesn't like **TrueType** and you have to use it, outline it (select the text, go to the Type menu, and choose "Create Outlines").

- Check every page to ensure there are **no empty frames** hanging around (only because it's like having dirty socks all over the floor when company comes over): From the View menu, go down to Extras and choose, "Show Frame Edges." If you see any empty frames, delete them.

Also check the Preflight panel, as shown on page 214, then package your files (page 215) or make a PDF for print (page 216).

Check the press specs

The printing specifications for various projects have been mentioned here and there throughout this book, but I've made a table for easy reference, below.

	Desktop Printer	Commercial Press
document **size**	Depends on the paper tray in your printer. Check your manual.	Start at the end—that is, the printer determines the size of your document. Check the web site or call the press.
document **bleed**	Not many desktop printers can print bleeds, so you must design with that in mind.	Almost always provide a bleed, even if you don't use it. Add one-eighth inch around all edges, generally. Check with the printer. See page 4.
color model of images and text	Low-end desktop printers don't care. If you have a high-end desktop printer, you probably care, so check the manual.	Always use CMYK. See pages 132 and 164–165.
resolution of images	Even on low-end desktop printers, a very low-resolution file, such as 72 ppi (typical of phone photos) will be fuzzy. Try to use at least 150 ppi for print.	Always use 300 ppi. You can get away with a little less, perhaps even down to 225, but try to stay around 300 ppi. See pages 133 and 149.
fonts	Low-end printers don't really care what font formats you use, and most high-end printers won't either. But even so, PostScript or OpenType formats are generally safer than TrueType.	The only problem format is TrueType, especially old TrueType. If you have a TrueType font you really have to use, change it to outlines., just to be safe. See page 187.

Check the Preflight panel

The Preflight panel is great. You might have seen a tiny message in the bottom-left corner telling you there are "No errors" or "17 errors." That's the Preflight panel constantly checking your document to make sure it's printable. It has its own defaults that it checks, but you can create customized profiles so it checks what *you* want it to check. For instance, for my jobs that go to a high-end press, such as this book, I tell the Preflight panel to make sure all my graphics are CMYK, of a certain resolution, the links are good, no fonts are missing, etc.

TASK 1   Check out the Preflight panel

1   There are two easy ways to open the Preflight panel:

- Click on the very tiny triangle in the bottom-left corner of the window, as shown below, to pop up the menu. Choose "Preflight Panel."

- *Or* from the Window menu, slide down to "Output," and then choose "Preflight."

2   This opens the Preflight panel that tells you what is wrong with your document, according to its defaults.

Your custom profile will appear here.

Click on the page number to go directly to that item so you can fix it.

3   To customize the panel, go to the Preflight panel menu and choose "Define Profiles…," *or* choose "Define Profiles…" from the pop-up menu as shown in Step 1.

Click the **+** button to add a new profile. Name it, and disclose each of the headings and make your selections. If you don't know what something is, leave it alone.

Package your files

When sending your files off to be printed, you need to include the InDesign file itself, of course, plus every graphic that is linked to the file, plus the fonts. To make this process so easy, InDesign has a Package feature. It gathers up everything it needs and puts *copies* of everything into a new folder, with the word "folder" at the end of the name.

In the process of packaging, InDesign does a preflight check, similar to the one you can do yourself on the opposite page. If you did a good job cleaning up your file and doing a preflight, there should be no errors in the packaging.

TASK 2 Package your file

1 From the File menu, choose "Package…." You'll see this dialog box:

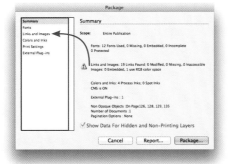

The warning symbol indicates there is an issue. In this case, the file accidentally includes an RGB graphic.

Click the appropriate heading in the sidebar to see specifically what the problem is.

2 If there are errors, as shown above, click the heading in the sidebar to see what the problems are. If they can't be fixed by selecting the file and clicking the "Update" button, you have to cancel this and go back to the InDesign file and fix it.

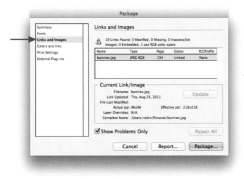

Click the button, "Show Problems Only," to pinpoint the issue.

If there are no issues, click "Package…" and let InDesign do its work.

NOTE: As mentioned above, InDesign puts a *copy* of everything in the packaged folder, so now you have duplicates of every little thing in that file. You might want to delete the original folder in which you were storing most of these files, but first check to make sure you don't throw out some great graphics that you thought you were going to use, but didn't.

Export to PDF

If you have created a lovely piece and you either want to send it via email, post it online, or upload it to an online print shop for printing, you can create a PDF very quickly in InDesign.

1 From the File menu, slide down to "Adobe PDF Presets."

2 Of the options in the submenu, choose the one appropriate for the destination of the PDF:

- If the PDF is to be viewed on a screen of any sort, choose "Smallest File Size…."

- If you're sending the PDF to someone to print on her desktop printer, choose "High Quality Print…."

- If you are sending this job to a high-end press and they have told you to send a press-quality file, choose "Press Quality…."

- If you're uploading the file to a print shop and their specs say to create a PDF/X-4, then, of course, choose "PDF/X-4…."

3 Name the file and save into a folder where you can find it again.

Now, that is the quick and easy way to make a PDF and will probably be sufficient for most of your needs. However, PDFs are hugely complex and mysterious and magical files. If you plan to produce a PDF for the press, get in touch with a representative of that press and make sure you are preparing the file appropriately. She may give you certain specifications to add to the dialog boxes before you save the file.

Save a file for earlier versions

InDesign doesn't have an option to save in an earlier version, but you can export any file as an "InDesign Markup" file. A file saved this way can be opened with a CS4 version of the program, although if it includes features that are specific to CS5 or CS5.5, those features (and perhaps the content) will be lost. The person running CS4 must make sure his app is completely up to date (go to the Help menu, choose "Updates…," and follow the directions).

1 From the File menu, choose "Export…."

2 At the bottom of the Export window, click the "Format" menu (PC: "File type" menu) and choose "InDesign Markup (IDML)."

3 Choose the folder in which to save the file, then click Save. The new file will have a **.idml** extension on the file name, instead of .indd.

If you need to take a file all the way back to CS3, you'll need to export it as an IDML file, open it in CS4, then from CS4, export it in the Interchange INX format.

Save a corrupted file

Sometimes a file starts crashing InDesign and you don't know why. The first thing to try is the technique mentioned above—**export the file as an IDML file,** then reopen it in InDesign. This has saved my boompah a number of times, including this very chapter file. Also try making a **snippet** of a page that you think is causing trouble, delete the original page, and replace with the snippet (see page 219).

Occasionally I have had files that crashed when creating an index or making a table of contents. I have been able to save the files by cleaning them up with the proverbial fine-tooth comb—getting rid of missing fonts that the file was still calling on, deleting unused style sheets, updating graphics, etc.

To prevent a file from crashing, this is the most important tip: Regularly do a "Save As" and replace the file. InDesign has almost unlimited Undos (the number of times you can undo something you just did). But it has to keep track of these in memory; when memory gets full, InDesign crashes and you risk corruption. So every time you do something big, such as delete pages, add pages, add or delete large graphics, or make global changes such as search-and-replace, save the file with the same name and replace it. Also "Save As" every hour or so. I can't stress enough how important this is to keep things running smoothly!

Where to go from here

As I've mentioned, this small book only touches the tip of the InDesign iceberg. I hope it makes you want to find out more! Here are a couple of great places to learn more about this great tool.

- **Help files:** Adobe's help files are pretty good. They include not only the entire manual (searchable), but links to people in the community who offer support, video tutorials from Adobe and others, and much more.

- *Real World Adobe InDesign CS5* (with free CS5.5 bonus content), an 800-page book by Olav Kvern, David Blatner, and Bob Bringhurst. If you can't find the info you need in that book, it doesn't exist. It's available from Peachpit Press.

- **Adobe InDesign CS5: Learn by Video** series from Peachpit Press.

- *Before & After: How to Design Cool Stuff*
  You really must subscribe to *Before & After,* from John McWade. It's the best thing I've ever seen on design, and now you know enough about InDesign to understand and benefit from the concepts John talks about. He provides short bits on specific aspects of design, with brilliant examples and explanations. www.BAmagazine.com

- **The Non-Designer series,** from Peachpit Press. These books comprise a pretty good education in the basics of design, plus the basics of using the Adobe Creative Suite software:

  The Non-Designer's Design Book
  The Non-Designer's Type Book
  The Non-Designer's Presentation Book
  The Non-Designer's InDesign Book
  The Non-Designer's Photoshop Book (by John Tollett; I helped)
  The Non-Designer's Illustrator Book (by John Tollett; I helped)

  Plus these more advanced books:

  Robin Williams Design Workshop (with John Tollett)

  Robin Williams Handmade Design Workshop:
      Create Handmade Elements for Digital Design
      (my most favorite book ever, by Carmen Sheldon, and I helped)

Things yet to know!

Sadly, this small book does not do justice to the depth of InDesign. Here are *a few* other things I use all the time. To learn more about these, check the resources listed on the opposite page.

Paragraph Rules: I *love* paragraph rules. They are lines/strokes that you can attach to text. Every heading in this book that has a dotted line beneath it is using a paragraph rule; it is built into that style sheet so I just type and the dotted line appears. In fact, paragraph rules are dividing each of the paragraphs on this page (and nested styles that format the words in front of the colons automatically).

More on the Pen tool: The Pen tool is amazingly useful and it would be worth your time to learn it well.

Layers: InDesign has a Layers panel that makes it easy to create variations of a job and to organize lots of pieces. The layers are similar to the layers in Photoshop, except they do not interact with each other.

Spell Check: InDesign's spell check can check many different languages, and you can create your own user dictionary. Turn on Dynamic Spelling (from the Edit menu) so typos are fixed while you write.

Find and Change (search and replace): The Find/Change feature (in the Edit menu) is very powerful. Not only can you search for text and formatting, you can also search for object formatting as well, such as 3-point red strokes and change them to 4-point green strokes. If you know what GREP is, you can search with GREP.

Notes: You can attach notes to your work, either to remind you of things to do or to add comments for your client or to share a job with your coworkers, etc. They are quite powerful. Get "Notes" from the Type menu.

Preferences: Be sure to poke around in the Preferences panes!

Snippets: Select everything on your page and drag it to the Desktop; InDesign creates a *snippet* with the extension of .IDMS. Send this to someone else who uses InDesign (along with any linked graphics) and she can drag it onto an InDesign page, on which the snippet completely recreates itself. If you're having trouble with corruption, this can sometimes help clean up a file.

Object styles: Just like paragraph styles, you can create object styles to quickly format graphics. For instance, you might want a light drop shadow and a half-point black stroke on every photograph in your brochure; make that an object style and apply it with a click. Get the Object Styles panel from Window > Styles.

Guides: You can change the colors of the guides, which can be very useful. For instance, when working on a page that is completely covered by a graphic, you can change your guides to a very pale gray and choose to show them in front so you can see them.

Anchored objects: The little blue square on a text frame lets you attach, or anchor, any object (including another text frame) to a text frame. You might want to insert a photo directly into the text, as shown on page 87, or let it float outside the frame and move along with the text as you edit, as shown above-right. Just hover over the blue square and read its tool tip to learn how to use it. If you want to remove it, from the Object menu, choose Anchored Object > Release.

Import options: Both text files and graphic files have import options in which you can customize the file as you bring it in. To get the options, check the box in the Place dialog box, "Show Import Options."

Index